THE ART &
BUSINESS
OF WRITING

A Practical Guide to the Writing Life

THE ART & BUSINESS OF WRITING

A Practical Guide to the Writing Life

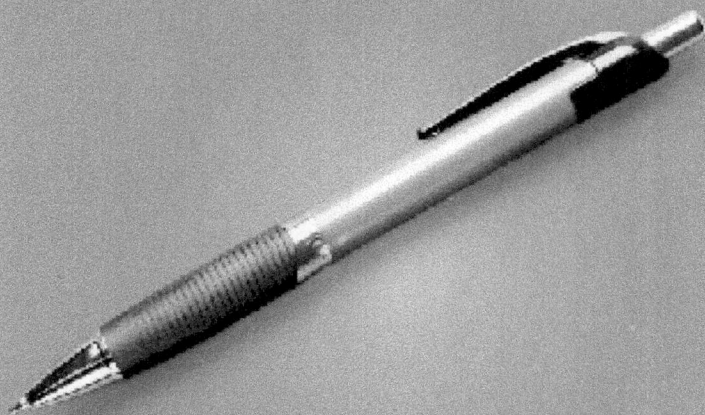

CHRIS JONES

Printed in the United States of America

ISBN 13: 9780692603703

First Edition

10 9 8 7 6 5 4 3 2 1

DEDICATION

To every aspiring author:

Your stories matter.

Share them.

CONTENTS

SECTION 3: Promoting Your Brand

INTRODUCTION

On March 23, 2016, my publisher fired me as editor-in-chief of his magazine. It was sudden—no warning, no reason. When I got the news—despite the shock—I didn't panic. I called my wife. "I've been fired," I said, "but we'll be all right."

That statement wasn't a defense mechanism. It was the truth. Until that point, I had kept an updated resignation letter in the top right drawer of my desk. I intended to submit it on June 30. My boss beat me to the punch. Until that day, I was hard at work in the evenings growing a base of clients for a writing business I intended to launch on July 1. That unexpected termination meant it was go time—sink or swim, baby.

I sifted through my contact list and reached out to people who had opportunities available that I could not capitalize on as an employee. Right off the bat, I got an ongoing writing gig with a local magazine, picked up some assignments from a regional magazine, and was offered a content editing contract from a small business. Within a few months, I got another freelance writing post with another regional magazine. To what did I owe it all? My network.

Writers write. We know that. If you're reading this book, you're already writing or searching for your jump-off point. One of the best things you can do as a writer is to keep busy at your craft and develop relationships with people who you think could have an interest in your work or know someone who does. Everything rises and falls on the strength of our platform and our network.

One of the saddest realities about writing is the outside

world's perception of our work. Most people are clueless. When I go to parties or get-togethers and tell people I write for a living, I get that Nick Cannon meme face. You know, the one where Nick's head is tilted sideways, mouth gaped open, and his eyebrows cocked in complete bewilderment? That face. "Oh," they say. People pigeonhole writers into two larg categories: novelists and starving novelists. They don't know how far and wide writing goes. It's everywhere, from the movies they watch on Netflix to the content they consume in magazines and on websites. Yet, it doesn't dawn on them that writers produce content they enjoy. "The president's speech was fantastic," someone across the room will say. "I had to grab the instruction manual to fix the microwave last week," quips another. "Have you seen Hamilton? It's amazing," spouts someone else. All oblivious to the fact that writers created it all. And it's our job to educate them.

On my podcast, *The Art & Business of Writing*, I had the pleasure of interviewing two writers from different walks—Joanna Penn and Eric Rosenberg. Joanna is a full-time author making six figures writing fiction novels, nonfiction books and through speaking. Millions download her podcast, *The Creative Penn*. Eric Rosenberg, a six-figure writer, and podcaster at *Personal Profitability*, got his start writing on finance blogs. He maintains that niche to this day. Would anyone say they're not successful? James Cook is credited with saying, "A man who wants to lead the orchestra must first turn his back on the crowd." You, writer, therefore, must ignore doubters, the ignorant, and those who minimize your work. Writing is more than a hobby; it's a lucrative career if you have the drive, determination, and willingness to burn the ships on the shore and conquer your fears.

Do you accept the challenge? If you do, I'll walk you through developing your writer's mindset, help you choose the tools of the trade, teach you the basics of creating your website, and share ways to promote yourself at networking events and online. In the Appendix, I've added bonus material to give you the boost you need to succeed.

Your creative gift is meant to be shared. Word by word, I hope you'll embrace your creative life and, who knows, if you apply what you learn here, you too may leap from blank page to bookstore shelf. Are you ready? Then let's go!

BECOMING A WRITER

"Writing is an exploration. You start from nothing and learn as you go." - E. L. Doctorow

CHAPTER 1
AFFIRMATIONS FOR INSPIRATION

In the film *The Lord of the Rings: The Fellowship of the Ring*, Samwise Gamgee agrees to join his friend, Frodo Baggins, on the journey of a lifetime through Middle Earth to Mount Doom to destroy the One Ring. As they approached the edge of the Shire, Samwise realizes the comfort of his present life would end. Stopping in the middle of the field, he says, "This is it. If I take one more step, it will be the farthest away from home I have ever been." Frodo turns to him, places his hands on his shoulder, smiles, and says, "Come on." And they begin their epic journey.

If you're ready to write and embark on an incredible writing journey, then it's time to take that next step. Leave your comfort and security behind and let's go. The little voice will tell you it's scary—and it is—and that you have no business "leaving the Shire," but like Samwise, you have a dream, you crave fulfillment, and that means going places you've never been before to do things you've never done. That's the writing life. It starts with learning to affirm yourself and to quiet that little voice so you can keep you placing one foot in front of the other until you get there.

When I returned to full-time writing after several inactive years, my first order of business was to change my belief system. I had to decide how I wanted to show up as a writer and what my relationship to the craft would be. I achieved this by writing affirmations to read throughout my day.

It doesn't matter how talented a writer you are, something within—that unrelenting little voice—whispers, You're unworthy, or You're untalented, or You're unqualified to write. Julia Cameron, author of the bestselling book *The Artist's Way*, calls this The Censor. Steven Pressfield, who wrote the bestselling book *The War of Art*, refers to it as Resistance and others call it Imposter's Syndrome. No matter what you call it, it's not worthy of an audience—at least not in the beginning.

When you're starting, that small voice beats the drum of your fears and insecurities about writing every time you sit down to create. It heckles you with thoughts like, "Calling yourself a writer now, eh?" or "Who wants to read anything you write?" or "What new do you have to say that hasn't already been said?" Worst of all, it throws this nasty dagger: "What if you fail?" Every writer from J. K. Rowling to Stephen King deals with this. The little voice never goes away. It's relentless, but as you write, you'll learn to recognize its voice and learn how to make it help you. Cec Murphey, who ghostwrote Dr. Ben Carson's *Gifted Hands*, takes a different approach. He says he asks his inner critic to let him finish writing and then it can point out all the flaws it wants and claims to see. Not a bad approach, right?

Testing the Power of Thought

We're shaped by our thoughts, and the way we process our thoughts gives us the power to create success or produce failure. Try this exercise: recall a time when you felt most confident. Where were you? What were you were doing? Who were you spending time with? What caused your confidence? As you remember this time in your life, did you sense a shift in your mood? Did you feel that same confidence come over you again? Now consider a low point in your life. It may be the loss of a job, a relationship, or the death of a loved one. What happened? How did it make you feel? Who was there? What did you see? Did you notice a change in your state? It's a simple exercise I learned from Tony Robbins, and it's easy to see how much power our thoughts command. During the creative process, we'll want to tap into this power and use it to create momentum. We want to teach our minds to work for us and not against us. Reciting daily affirmations aloud helps to harness this power. You noticed what your mind could do in a matter of seconds with simple prompting. Let's learn to do it over a lifetime.

How to Write Affirmations

Written affirmations teach us to internalize future success in terms of completed tasks (i.e., I will create my author website by September 1). They challenge our brains to double down on focus and to work toward producing the desired outcome. My first affirmation was allowing myself to pursue writing again: "I give myself permission to write." I affirmed my talent and support system next: "I am a talented writer. My loved ones support my decision to write." I affirmed my state of mind for writing, too: "I wake up every morning excited to write." Whatever you affirm, write three to five affirmations, and reread them throughout the day, speaking them out loud when possible. Set alerts on your phone reminding you to read them if you must. It doesn't matter if you believe them today, in time you will. As your deadline-based affirmations pass, you'll want to create new affirmations to replace those (i.e., I will publish my novel on December 1). Writing can be emotionally taxing. Using affirmations to keep you progressing upward builds strong mental and emotional resolve to keep you on the page during those low points—and they come!

When you write and then read daily, "I will create my author's website by September 1," you make an internal commitment to achieve the outcome by the chosen date. Your brain then goes about figuring out how it will achieve this goal, and which steps you'll need to take. It asks, "Which platform will I use for my website?", "Where will I host it?", "What will my domain name be?", "Should I find help designing it?" Write down your action steps and the subsequent action steps needed to hit those milestones. This saves you from overwhelm down the road, especially if life gets in the way or if you procrastinate. You'll always know what's next. Once written, read your affirmations daily. Reciting them helps you to visualize the outcome with clarity. You'll feel resistant—and a little silly—about doing them at first but keep going.

In addition to attaching goals to your affirmations, anchor them with emotion. When you link a strong enough emotion to a goal, you increase your likelihood of reaching it. Imagine dialing up your website in a browser window. See yourself navigating the pages. Visualize the layout of each page. Imagine when you finally share a link with friends and followers on social media. Now, doesn't that put you into an excited state? Why? Because it's something you've wanted, and you can now start to see it. Now do you see how powerful affirmations can be?

Keep Your Affirmations Visible

Affirmations work when you can see them. Here are ways to manage yours for quick recall:

- **Voice recording.** Record them and listen to them throughout the day—when you exercise, on a car ride, or right before you go to sleep. Recording them is as simple as using the pre-installed voice recorder on your smartphone.

- **Stick them up.** Tape them to a mirror, your computer monitor, your desk, your fridge, or on your car's dashboard. You don't have to list them all in one place. Post one here and one there in areas you visit frequently.
- **Email them.** Send yourself automated emails at a certain time each day. Boomerang for Gmail is one such program (boomeranggmail.com). It allows you to schedule when emails go out from your inbox. Keep your affirmations in a draft folder and paste them into emails scheduling them to go out throughout the day.
- **Set reminders.** Use a reminder app with an alarm. Wunderlist (wunderlist.com) and even the native reminders app on your phone works well and allow for recurring notifications. Whichever app you choose, commit to it.
- **Memorize them.** Use flashcards to jot down your affirmations and then commit them to memory. Memorization helps fight off negative self-talk that creeps into your head at any given moment.
- **Place them in your purse or wallet.** Write them on a small sheet of paper and store them for easy retrieval.
- **Make a song.** It's no coincidence that children learn through song. "Twinkle, Twinkle Little Star," "The Alphabet Song," and "Baa Baa Black Sheep" all use the same tune. If it works for tots, it can work for you.

> I will write my book this year,
> That's my goal, and it is clear,
> Write it, edit it, lay it out,
> That's what being an author's about.

- **Use a journal.** Write them daily in your journal or the margin of the page.

Your First Affirmations

Let's put it to the test and get started with your first affirmations. On a sheet of paper or in a note-taking app, write down five affirmations.

TAKEAWAYS

1. Success in writing involves having a powerful and purposeful thought life. With our thoughts, we can set and smash our writing goals, or we can succumb to the negative dialogue within. Instead of bending to it, we should harness it and learn to use it.

2. Affirmations are one of the best ways to help you keep focus and to control negative thoughts. Having a few of these written and recited daily can bring us into a resourceful mindset.

3. Put your affirmations in visible areas or use your devices to remind you to review them throughout the day when you will need the pick me up.

CHAPTER 2

Journaling Starts the Journey

Before indoor plumbing, you pumped water from a well. You'd march to the well, bucket in hand, grab the handle, and pump it until the water spewed from the nozzle.

At first, the water expelled by the nozzle isn't drinkable— it's murky, brown, and smelly from settling. After pumping for a minute, clear, cold water emerges. That's how journaling works. It's sitting down at your desk for twenty to thirty minutes to prime your pump. Don't expect it to be fluid like a diary. It's not supposed to be. It's designed to help you open your creative flow and can serve other purposes. Journaling over the years has helped solve problems within my writing, answer questions within my relationships, provided ideas for my business, and decluttered my mind so I could write clearly. If you've read the bestselling book *The Artist's Way*, you're likely familiar with what author Julia Cameron calls Morning Pages. Same concept.

I would be remiss if I didn't address a long-standing problem I sometimes face with journaling—morning haze. There are times when I open my journal and stare at the blank pages.

Even the stream-of-consciousness dries up—a wordless bed. When that happens, I walk.

Walking opens your mental flow. I start at a moderate pace while taking in deep breaths. It's meditative. I recite my affirmations, notice and enjoy my surroundings, pray, listen to music, or fire up a podcast. The end game is to open my mind and shake out the cobwebs. Within twenty minutes, I'm usually ready to journal.

Not much of a morning mover? You can substitute anything non-creative. Brew coffee, read, straighten up your writing desk, or cook breakfast. Find what works for you and make use of it.

Let's Get Started

Grab a notebook, a pen, and schedule twenty to thirty minutes each morning. Don't overthink it. Crack open your journal and write. Capture every thought. Sometimes your entries may be all gibberish, and that's okay. Prime your pump; open your mind for creative flow and thought exploration. If an idea worth exploring wanders onto your page, circle it and place in a separate notebook or note-taking app to revisit after you've finished writing. Your goal here is to not stop the flow of words.

My 100-Day Challenge

When I started journaling, I wanted to test its power by giving my first journaling experience a fixed amount of time—100 days. I chose 100 days because it was a strong psychological milestone number—we commemorate 100-year anniversaries, television shows and podcasts celebrate their 100th episodes, and some people hope to live to 100 years old, and so forth. Once you commit to a time frame, decide what you want your writing to accomplish. When I started this practice in 2011, my goal was to return to full-time writing after seven years off.

After 75 days, the idea for a blog showed up on my page. I explored that in a separate notebook as I continued to write daily. Before long, I had a blog set up and within three months, I was noticed by a local magazine. Six months later, I became its editor.

As you can see, having a clearly defined goal is the most important step. It gives your mind a target. If your goal is a book, say so. If you want to begin a freelance writing career, express it. Whatever goal you have for journaling, bring that intention to your pages each morning. You don't have to write about your goal, but it must run in the background. Stay faithful to this exercise, and before long, you'll see progress if you trust the process.

TAKEAWAYS

1. Establishing the practice of daily journaling helps to open creative flow. It gets your mind focused early on writing.

2. Journaling doesn't have to be beautiful or perfectly done, but it should become your practice. Focus on sifting out the dirt and catching the golden nuggets that come forth.

3. Use a separate journal for exploring ideas that show up on your pages. Are there ideas you can use in your work?

4. Set a goal and challenge yourself to write about that goal for 100 days to see what becomes of it.

CHAPTER 3

Creating a Habit

Whenever I sit on panel discussions at writer's conferences and at my book festival, someone always asks how often a writer should write. The short answer is daily. Every writer is different, and your life circumstances and work schedule play a factor, but if you can make time to write daily, do so. Make it a non-negotiable habit the same as going to the gym, taking a class, or learning a new skill.

Imagine asking your doctor, personal trainer, or dietitian how long you should maintain a balanced diet and exercise. You'd get a funny look. Health is a lifestyle and not a destination. It's the same with being a writer. It's who you are, not what you do. So, treat your writing with the professional courtesy it deserves. You're no different from a basketball player who needs to practice throughout the week to be game-ready or a ballerina who needs to work on her routine for hours a day to be prepared for a recital. Even if you don't write, touch your work: edit a sentence or a paragraph, research the next section of your book, flesh out a character, but above all else, show up.

Once we settle the how often question, the next hand ascending from the crowd asks: How much should I write every day?

A common rule of thumb in writing circles is 500 words per day. I've known writers who write 5,000 words a day. That's not for me, and it may not be for you. I recommend finding a comfortable number to see how it works for you for a week, two weeks, or a month. Track your output daily and take the average at the end of your chosen time frame. Test whether that number works for you, or if you were more consistent with a higher or lower number. You can always increase your word count over time.

I also recommend experimenting with writing time. You may prefer writing in the morning before your day begins than later when you may be tired from work.

Building your writing muscle is like weight training. You start with smaller weights and progress to heavier weights when you get stronger. Whatever number and time you select, aim to stick with it. Put it in your calendar and make that time non-negotiable. In time, you'll go from 500 words per day to 1,000 and from 1,000 to 3,000 or more. But that starts with developing a consistent, daily writing habit.

While we're discussing habits, I understand that sometimes getting started is hard to do. Here are a few ways to get your mind moving when you're not sure what to write or when you're between writing projects.

Writing Prompts

Writing prompts give you a subject or situation to write about to get your creative engine revved up in ten to fifteen minutes. Here are a few resources online that offer writing prompts:

- **Writer's Digest** (writersdigest.com/prompts): Get hundreds of writing prompts to help you work your mental muscle.

- **Creative Writing Prompts** (creativewriting-prompts. com/creative-writing-prompts): This website has over 60 writing prompts with links to more. This site is ideal for the writer who isn't working on a project and wants to maintain the practice.
- **Grammarly**   (grammarly.com/blog/fun-writing-prompts): These prompts will get your mind engaged and ready to write like stretches before a jog.
- **Reedsy**   (blog.reedsy.com/creative-writing-prompts): Reedsy offers over 1,0000 writing prompts to stimulate creativity. Submit your prompts for a chance to win in weekly cash contests.

If writing prompts aren't your cup of tea, you can use one of my favorites—writing sprints.

Writing Sprints

I love track and field. During the Summer Olympics, you can find me glued to my television watching the runners. I'm amazed at how they get focused, position themselves into their lanes, and when the gun sounds—whoosh! Off they go for just a few seconds until they cross the finish line.

Writers have an exercise much like this and by the same name—writing sprints. While there is no track, it involves the same principles of focusing, getting in your lane, and bolting when the gun sounds.

Sprints are a pressure-based exercise that forces writers to stop thinking and start writing. You set a timer—twenty-five minutes per sprint—and write as many words as you can until the alarm sounds. If you're sprinting with others online—within a Facebook Group or on Twitter—you report and repeat until the agreed number of sprints ends, or your schedule permits no more writing time. If you want to see chatter about sprints, log on to Twitter and use #writingsprints to the feed. It's surprising how fun and productive virtual writing can be. The best benefit to sprinting is the connections you'll make along the way with other writers, something valuable for the journey.

There will be times when you'll want to sprint and may not find companions. When I'm doing my sprints without people from Twitter or Facebook, I turn to my next device—a Pomodoro timer.

The Pomodoro Technique

Francesco Cirillo developed the Pomodoro Technique in the late 1980s. It breaks down work into twenty-five-minute intervals, separated by five-minute breaks designed to improve mental agility, allowing the brain to rest between uninterrupted stretches of work. This technique works in response to our natural reaction to Parkinson's Law, which states that work expands to fill time. If the time we allot is twenty-five minutes, we apply our energies to ensuring that we produce results in that time frame. It's a mind hack that will get your pen moving or your fingers pecking. You can find Pomodoro apps in your Google Play or iPhone App store. I use Flow. It's minimalist and has a MacBook taskbar companion. It allows me to shut off apps I choose for focused writing. Try a few of the apps in your store to see which suits you. You can even set your intervals to times that are suitable for your available time to write as well. Twenty-five minutes is the default setting, but you can set yours to best suit how you write.

When to Write

As important as how often to write and how much to write is when to write. My only advice: find your best writing time and lock it into your calendar. Let's look at the possibilities you might consider.

Late Nights. For a season, I tried to write deep into the night. I would come home from my day job as a magazine editor, play with my children, eat dinner, decompress, and spend time with my wife. Then around 9 p.m., I would retreat to the kitchen table with my laptop and write, blog, and manage my social profiles. I enjoyed the quiet of the night, but in time, inconsistency caused by fatigue from the day, needing to devote attention to my wife, or managing other matters interfered with my writing time. I concluded that writing at night wasn't good for me at all. It compromised my best energy and productivity. I could, however, dictate at night without losing a step, and I used that time to record what I would like to get down on paper. This has saved me in two ways: 1) it gets words out of my head when I'm too tired to write them, and 2) it provides a platform on which to build the next day. I never have to worry about what I will write about; it's waiting for me. You might find that writing at night works for you. I know several writers who do their writing late in the evening.

Early Mornings. After experimenting with night writing, I gave morning writing a go. Many of my friends on Instagram were writing in the morning and doing so with measurable success. I got up at 5:45 a.m. to run by 6:15 a.m. After my run, I journaled, and then I wrote. I was fresher in the morning than I was at night and could better engage with my book. I didn't have to concern myself with the fatigue or interruption that encroached on my night writing. It's easy to see why personal trainers tell you to hit the gym in the morning. Once done, I finished for the day and if I wrote later in the day, that was bonus time. I also found that my creative energy was stronger and more focused the earlier I started. I could write for one to two hours without being mentally fatigued.

Whether you fancy yourself an owl or a lark, choose the best time for you based on your lifestyle and schedule and put it on your calendar. Having set times in stone increases the likelihood that you'll commit.

What to Do If You Get Writer's Block

I used to subscribe to the myth of writer's block. What I thought was a creative barrier was my mind dividing focus between writing and solving other internal or external conflicts in my life (i.e., worrying about money, thinking about a deadline, fighting situational depression). Think back to the last time you dealt with what you perceived as writer's block. Was it? Or were other external factors affecting your ability to focus on writing?

I recognize that sometimes our creative drive gets stuck in park, but we are far from blocked. In those moments, we need to take action to snap ourselves back into a writing focus. Here are a few remedies to use when the words aren't flowing:

- **Walking.** A brisk twenty-minute stroll gets your heart rate up and your mind active.
- **Gaming.** I keep a few mobile phone games handy when I need a quick zap of stimulation. Recently, a friend gifted me with a Raspberry Pi fully loaded with retro games from my childhood. After a twenty-minute game break, I can usually get back to the page.
- **Cleaning.** Ever notice how creative you get when you're doing non-creative tasks like cleaning? Ideas seem to flow when my hands are submerged in dishwater or pushing a lawn mower.
- **Coloring.** There's a reason adult coloring book sales surged a few years ago. Art is therapeutic. I keep a coloring book and a sketchpad in my office for doodling in during low focus times.

- **Conversation.** I'm most energized after meeting a friend for coffee or after talking to a business associate or fellow writer. Build in some time during your week for meaningful chatter. Even a casual conversation with a neighbor across yards does the trick.
- **Sleeping.** Sometimes there is no way around the need for a nap. Set an alarm for twenty- or thirty-minute power naps and recharge.
- **Exercise.** I don't know a single person who doesn't get a boost of energy after a workout. Jump some rope, curl some weights, or do yoga.
- **Music.** I like to listen to the same song, or album, on repeat for hours. The catch with this is the song must have a repetitive beat or a catchy chorus (e.g., *Sweet Dreams* by Beyonce, *Bolero* by David Garrett, *Save Your Tears* by The Weeknd). Not all writers can work to music, but if you can, give this mind hack a try. (Bonus tip: Create writing playlists on Spotify or Apple Music and train your mind to write when they're played!)
- **Driving.** Hop in the car and explore an unfamiliar stretch of road. Venturing into the unknown gets the mind into a curious and creative space.

We create habits through repetition and writing is no different. Protect your writing time, and your creativity will reward you. Get the conviction that your writing deserves to be taken as seriously as your workout, your job, and your relationships. Let your goals drive you, your writing inspire you, and your calendar keep you accountable.

TAKEAWAYS

1. Write daily and make it a non-negotiable activity the same you would going class, work, or to the gym.

2. Creating your writing routine takes some experimentation. Try as many methods as you can until you find what works for you.

3. Use writing prompts or writing sprints to get your creative juices flowing when you have a slow creative drain.

4. Figure out your best writing time and make it a date!

5. Writing is your profession and not your hobby. Treat it with the same professionalism you would your job.

CHAPTER 4

Developing Your Book Idea

In a 2016 blog post, author and publishing consultant Jane Friedman lamented, "I'm astounded by the number of authors who come to me for coaching who admit that they don't read the genre they're writing in."

I'm assuming that's not you, and I'll move beyond the lecture of how to choose your genre (hint: it's most likely the one you read and enjoy the most). Friedman asserts, "Though it's not a prerequisite that you be fully educated about the genre you're entering, reading the best-selling authors who've come before you and brushing up on the craft specific to your genre will give you a leg up."

I agree. Writing what you know will keep you motivated, inspired, and authentic—and readers know when a writer loves their subject and when they're trying to make a quick buck. (Note: The money comes, but it's a by-product of giving your reader a world-class experience with your book.)

When deciding my genre, I knew I read nonfiction how-to and self-help almost exclusively. I enjoyed teaching writing, and I had a healthy interest in marketing and promotion, something spanning back to my days as a graphic designer. As I perused forums online and chatted with other writers, my target market confirmed the need for the information I knew. This pivoted my half-written book on writing creative nonfiction into the book you're reading now.

I scoured the Internet for the right method for developing my book outline and found three methods: avatar-based, Point A to Point B, and Scrum. I tried all three with varying degrees of success, and I recommend you do the same to see which method works for you.

Using an Avatar to Target Your Audience

I picked this method up from Kate Erickson of Entrepreneur on Fire. She personifies her avatar making it the person who benefits most from her content. Take a moment to think of your ideal reader as a living, breathing person. On a sheet of paper, answer these questions:

- What is their name?
- What do they do for work (or where do they go to school)?
- Where do they live?
- What is their dream?
- How important is it to them to achieve their dream?
- What does their day look like (i.e., job, routine, etc.)?
- What's their pain point?
- Where do they look for solutions to solve their problems?
- Where do they access the right tools to help him or her take the next step?
- Who among your contemporaries do they already read?
- How will you solve their problem?

Meet my Avatar, Sarah

Sarah is twenty-four and lives in an apartment in the suburbs. She's a journalist for a local magazine and wants to build a platform of inspiring stories that resonate with her readers.

She loves to learn and listen to podcasts by Joanna Penn, Jeff Goins, and Marie Forleo while driving to work, when working out at the gym, or out on a run. Sarah also reads blogs aimed at writers and subscribes to email lists to get free tips and eBooks to improve her craft. She follows industry-thought leaders like Dave Chessen, Mark Dawson, and Amy Porterfield on social media and makes it a point to attend one writing conference each year.

In her free time, she's working on a book she hopes to self-publish. Sarah wonders if she will ever finish the book. She's been working on it for over a year. Her friends and family believe in her and often tell her she has the talent. Her biggest fear isn't writing the book, but how to publish, promote, and sell her book—and where to find the time to do it.

As you can see, this exercise is useful and fun. It gives you a person you can think about as you write. Erickson says as she creates, she talks to her avatar and asks her what she wants and decides her course of action based on her avatar's needs. It's a strategy that keeps you focused on your audience and their needs as you write your book.

The Point A to Point B Method

I learned this method from Darren Rowse at ProBlogger. In the Point A to Point B method, you draw a line down the center of a sheet of paper labeling the left side "A" and the right side "B." On side "A," list your targeting readers. On side "B," write how your book will grow, inspire, or entertain your readers. The "B" side shows whether your topic connects with your audience, or if it requires further thought to get them from A to B. I like this method to help to gauge the motivation for which we write. If the dots don't connect for me, I can't expect them to resonate with my reader either.

Scrum Method

I learned this technique from organization expert Linda Clevenger when she appeared on Episode 008 of my podcast. This method involves using post-it notes to construct your book from start to finish so you can outline it.

Begin by writing every topic you can think of regarding your book on separate notes. Let's say your book is about how to play basketball. On several notes, write the topics: equipment, rules, history, choosing a basketball, shoes, drills, playing defense, and so forth. Stick these up on a blank wall or a whiteboard. As you exhaust all your ideas, figure out where each fits in and if certain topics can serve as chapters. Grouping them up on the wall or the board creates chapters, sub-titles, and your table of contents. I recommend this method most. It's a great way to open your mind and get to the writing faster—plus it's fun. What's great about this is that you can use it to organize almost anything, from your goals to your business.

Takeaways

1. Create your avatar, a fictional person who represents your ideal reader. Make your avatar as real as possible.

2. When developing your book idea, spend some time getting all the knowledge you have about the subject matter out of your head to better organize ideas into themes.

3. Think about who your reader is and how your book solves their problems. Develop your idea around fixing the pain point of your reader based on your expertise.

CHAPTER 5

Setting the Pace With Word Counts

In the sports world, pitchers have pitch counts, basketball players have shot attempts, and running backs have carries. We writers? Our stat is the word count. In the spirit of not getting too caught up in measurements and metrics, and it's easy to do, I want to give you an idea of why it matters, and why it doesn't.

If you've been writing for any amount of time, you've heard of National Novel Writing Month (NaNoWriMo). If not, all you need to know is that every November writers from around the world pledge to write a 50,000-word novel in 30 days. This shakes out to 1,667 words per day. No pressure, right? While it works for some writers, it intimidates others. I enjoy using the contest to leverage its excitement. Who doesn't want to join a band of writers for a month of writing and talking writing across social media? While I've hit the 50,000-word mark once, I've not worried about it in recent years. I enjoy the camaraderie of writing with others toward a common goal for one month out of the year.

NaNoWriMo forces you to push out a book in a month and leaves you the following month for post-production—editing, proofreading, and polishing. While 50,000 words in one month is an aggressive schedule, let's deconstruct some ways you can write a book in a set time.

- If you want to write a book in 30 days, write 1,667 words per day.
- If you want to write a book in 60 days, write 834 words per day.
- If you want to write a book in 90 days, write 556 words per day.
- If you want to write a book in 6 months, write 277 words per day.
- If you want to write a book in 9 months, write 186 words per day.
- If you want to write a book in one year, write 137 words per day.

Eating the proverbial elephant one bite at a time, this breakdown makes it easy to remove excuses and write around any scenario in your life. At the minimum, you have a book in a year doing fewer than 150 words per day, which is far less than most people text message in an hour.

Focus on Narrative

I won't call word counts unimportant—I aim to have one for each book as a gauge—but I will say they're not a hard and fast rule. Your readers would prefer you write a good book at 25,000 words that's clean and concise than a 50,000-word book with fluff. When the book is done, it's finished. And it will tell you if you listen. Many of my favorite works are short on words but long on story. Here they are (page counts in parenthesis):

- *The Present* by Spencer Johnson (109)
- *Of Mice and Men* by John Steinbeck (112)

- *Running with the Giants* by John C. Maxwell (160)
- *The Go-Giver* by Bob Burg & David Mann (144)
- *The Greatest Salesman in the World* by Og Mandino (130)
- *Animal Farm* by George Orwell (113)

Write Cleanly and Don't Gump

Remember the film "Forrest Gump?" When the film should have ended, they treated us to Forrest running across the country and prolonged the film for another 30 minutes or more. That's what adding fluff to good work for the sake of reaching a word count does. Don't do it. Write cleanly. Trust your words. Listen to your book. Know your reader.

Takeaways

1. Word counts are important but serve as a guideline for writing more than a goal for completing a work. The goal should be a complete story at any word length.

2. Create a writing schedule and show up daily to your work. Time spent writing each day adds up and, in time, you'll have a completed book.

3. Confidence comes in doing. The more you write, the more likely you are to keep writing.

CHAPTER 6

Choosing the Right Writing Software

Writing and publishing books has never been easier. Services like Amazon's Kindle Direct Publishing (KDP) and Ingram Spark put industry-standard publishing options at your fingertips. All you must do is write, upload, and publish. Before we get ahead of ourselves, you first need to write your book. In this chapter, we'll examine the most used word processing tools and mobile apps to help you get that book from your head to the page. You may be familiar with some and not with others. That's all right. By the time we finish, you'll have a list of software and apps at your disposal to jump-start your writing.

Writing Software

While the list below is not an exhaustive list of software suites on the market, they represent applications I've used and tested. I'm not versed in others like Vellum or Ulysses, but I have heard good things about both.

Microsoft Word

Word is the flagship word processing software in Microsoft Office. It allows you to write, edit, and format books for publishing (though I don't recommend it). For Mac users, Word is plug-and-play, making it easy to download, install, and use. PCs come with a trial version of Word pre-installed. Chromebook and iPad users will need to go to their respective app stores to download and install Word. There is also a mobile app for writing on the go, which you'll find handy if you enjoy writing on a tablet or your phone. The mobile version syncs with your desktop version.

Pros:
- Word count tracking
- Page breaking for separating chapters
- Sidebar to review pages or outlines
- Review panel for collaboration
- Focus view for distraction-free writing.
- Mobile app
- Read Aloud feature for auditory editing
- Voice dictation
- Grammarly and ProWritingAid plug-in for self-editing

Cons:
- All chapters in one document
- Research must be kept in separate folders.
- A long history of software crashing
- Requires a license

My preference is to use Word for editing only. I have yet to find a more collaborative editing tool. Scores of writers enjoy writing in Word and if it works for your workflow, use it.

Google Docs

A favorite among Mac users, Google Docs has come a long way in closing the functionality gap between itself and Word. Past versions limited writers to typewriter-like word processing, but now it performs on par with Word. Google Docs is browser-based and free, which appeals to users with limited hard drive space and smaller budgets.

Pros:
- Browser-based (write from any computer by logging in to Google)
- Easy collaboration and document sharing
- Can integrate and convert Word documents
- Mobile app
- Voice dictation
- Grammarly plug-in for self-editing
- Can be used offline and synced when back online

Cons:
Except for occasional crashing, Google Docs shares the same cons as Word.

The simplicity of the app is something to be held in high esteem. Google Docs is neat and streamlined and, when working with an editor or collaborator, its comment bubbles are more pronounced than Word and easier to collaborate.

Scrivener

Scrivener has had a cult-like following for as long as I can remember. It wasn't until I completed NaNoWriMo 2014 that I used it and was surprised by its power. Scrivener allows you to build your entire book into separate chapters and compile research right within the interface. It even has pre-built templates for various types of books.

Pros:
- Binder panel for chapter-by-chapter reviewing
- Upload photos, audio clips, and videos into the interface
- Bookmarking for easy research recall
- Inspector sidebar for leaving notes about your document
- Voice dictation
- Mobile app
- Binder merge (for authors who like to work on multiple books)
- Compile feature organized book for formatting

Cons:
- No ability to collaborate
- Poor spelling/grammar check
- In-document formatting is difficult to get right
- Mobile app is not free ($19.99)

My recommendation: Scrivener. Its developer, Literature and Latte, also has training videos on its website to show you how to best use all the features of this robust writing software. It comes with a full 30-day trial, which equates to 30 use days and not 30 consecutive calendar days, like most trials.

I encourage you to try any of the applications above to see which one fits your writing style. What works for some writers doesn't work for all.

Mobile Apps

Mobile apps make writing on the go easier. Throughout the day, ideas come, and capturing those ideas is paramount. I have popped my phone open in line at the grocery store, during work breaks, when my children were on the playground, and during their soccer or baseball practices. These pockets of time turned into some of my most productive writing sessions, yielding an extra 500 to 1000 words. And once I discovered voice recording and transcribing, I captured even more words.

As mentioned in Chapter 3, it's imperative to guard your writing time as much as you can, but disruptions in life are inevitable. Since I mentioned Microsoft Word, Google Docs, and Scrivener's mobile apps earlier, I don't see fit to mention them again. Instead, I'll share a few apps I've used when inspiration strikes, and I need to make use of the time right away.

- **Evernote (evernote.com).** Evernote is a complete note-taking system. I have used it to jot down ideas, write sections and chapters of my book, and to flesh out concepts. It also comes with an audio recorder for dictation. Evernote has a desktop app and a web-based platform for syncing to its desktop companion, so nothing gets lost between devices. You can use the free version of Evernote or upgrade to premium versions starting at $7.99 per month, or $69.99 per year.
- **Rev (rev.com).** Rev allows you to voice record into its app and send your files for transcription. Its $1.25 per minute of audio price tag is inexpensive when you consider how many words you can speak in small pockets of time. The service guarantees 99% accuracy and a same-day turnaround for most audio uploads. If you don't want to pay for the audio transcription, you can use Transcribe (transcribe.wreally.com). This web-based tool allows you to upload your audio files and play them back at slower speeds for self-transcription. I've used this service ($20 per year for the license), and it's become an instrumental part of my writing workflow.
- **Temi (temi.com).** Like Rev, Temi allows you to record voice notes and upload them to be transcribed. The difference is where Rev is transcribed by humans, Temi is AI-based transcription service. This means accuracy can

go down—sometimes sharply, depending on how you speak. I recommend only using this service if you speak slowly and clearly, enunciating each of your words. The cost is 25 cents per minute. It offers a trial run to give you an idea of how it works in real time.

- **Dragon** (nuance.com). Much like the desktop application, the mobile app lets you dictate into your mobile device while it transcribes. It boasts a speed that's five times faster than typing on a keyboard. The desktop software (thought expensive) can learn the nuances of your voice for more accurate dictation.

These are a few of the many on the market. Some are easier and more user-friendly than others. It's up to you to find the one that best fits your workflow. I use a combination of Scrivener, Evernote, and Rev to get my work done, but you may find another combination to be more effective for you.

Takeaways

1. Don't allow time to become your excuse for not writing. There is plenty of time once you learn to recognize and use the small pockets available to you.

2. Find the writing suite and peripheral tools that work best for you and stick with them. Nothing will throw you off your flow like switching tools too often midstream.

3. If you find you like to write on the go, be sure the writing software you select has a mobile app so that you can sync your work across platforms (i.e., desktop, mobile, and tablet).

4. Make writing in small pockets of time your default setting.

CHAPTER 7

Organizing Your Ideas

"I read, I write, I think, I file." Those four governing daily principles outlined by John C. Maxwell in his book, Today Matters, transformed my life. Maxwell says by adhering to these principles, he's able to keep a steady stream of inspiration for his writing. When I applied them, I got the same result. From blog posts and marketing emails to magazine ad design and whatever I could capture, I kept in a file. The more I could catalog to inspire me, the better. But you may wonder: what is a swipe file anyway? Let's unpack it.

What is a Swipe File & Why Do You Need It?

A swipe file is a collection of written and visual material that a writer can use in a book or other writing projects when the need arises. I keep a stocked pond of inspirational quotes, magazine articles, email newsletters, social media graphics, book covers and layouts, and blog posts. Here are other items you can stash away for future use:

- Magazine stories with sources you can reference in books
- Cartoons
- Quotes
- Memes
- Data (e.g., charts, information, statistics, infographics)
- Photos (I've seen fiction authors do this when they see an image of someone who is the inspiration for a character)
- Full videos and social media video clips
- Audio clips and podcasts
- Lead generation tools (e.g., checklists, eBooks, and tip sheets I've opted in to receive)
- Eye-catching or trendy marketing material
- Fonts
- Headshot styles (for your future marketing)
- Press releases

Long story short, anything inspiring to you and your writing, marketing, or promotional efforts should be saved. You don't have to know how to design the art, just what resonates with your brand and your audience. These clips of inspiration can then be given to your designer, marketing person, or PR rep to draw inspiration from for you.

Swipe Filing Methods

There is no right or wrong method to swipe filing. I swipe electronically and organize hard copies of files in a folder that lives in a desk drawer. You may prefer Pinterest, Evernote, Milanote, or another way of organizing and arranging your swipe file. Let's explore the options.

- **Pinterest (pinterest.com).** Pinterest boards are an easy method to collect and save material. You can create public boards or keep your swipes to yourself with secret boards. If you download and install the browser widget, you can pin inspiration from around the Internet with the click of a button. Pinterest mobile allows you to snap images from your phone camera for quick import. Pinterest is chock full of creators who post a never-ending stream of content that you can pin to any of your boards. One children's book author I know found her book illustrator while browsing Pinterest. So, who knows, you might find your next illustrator or cover designer while storing ideas.

- **Trello (trello.com).** Trello uses the Kanban method of organizing to create visual dashboards. This system organizes your swipes into cards that you can arrange onto boards in any way you choose. Trello links to Google Drive and Dropbox for easy uploading. Once your file is uploaded, you can drag and drop the card to arrange your material by category or theme, use labeling to organize, and add or upload notes and supporting documents within each card you create for a robust filing experience.

- **Milanote (milanote.com).** Milanote is Trello meets Pinterest. Milanote allows you to create cards for various types of files (e.g., audio, video, image, color swatches, and more). They built it for creatives, and if you are an author who fancies visual book organization, you can build your fiction world, put all the assets for your book and cover on a board, create storyboards, outline blog posts, and many other visual functions. Milanote is my personal favorite.

Hard Copy Swipe Files

If you're the tangible type, you can always use the paper swipe file. Many public libraries allow you to purchase old magazines before they recycle them. Buy those magazines for a few shiny quarters and clip the inspiration out of them and place them in categorized manila folders. When reading books, copy down the quotes you like into a small notebook or onto index cards and save those index cards in the swipe file.

Swipe filing is an essential tool for writers. Use the best method for the results you want. Having research ready to go at your fingertips is invaluable. Sometimes I have sought a resource, like a quote or a story or a design idea, and I could scroll through my swipe file to find it. It's one of the most valuable assets to my writing, and if it's good enough for John C. Maxwell, who has published over 70 books and sold 20 million copies, it's good enough for me—and you.

Takeaways

1. Make swipe filing a daily habit. It's not only an easy way to keep a running collection of ideas, but it keeps your mind focused on the creative.

2. Choose an app that you find user-friendly and that works best for how you like and prefer to organize. Pinterest is the easiest jump-off point if you're new to swipe filing.

3. Keep a swipe file of things related to your current work in progress so you have the assets for later or to store away things for future projects.

CHAPTER 8

Balancing Your Writing Life

I worked with a business coach many years ago who helped me grow my web and graphic design company. In her training, I learned a lot about balance and singular focus. This involved examining which areas of my life were most important to my success and which activities would help me achieve it or detract from it. She used two exercises I want to pass on to you because I think they're essential to creating a well-balanced and productive writing lifestyle: the Wheel of Life and the Trivial Many and Vital Few.

The Wheel of Life

This exercise shows where you are in or out of balance. The goal is to identify eight areas of your life you deem most important to your well-being. The most chosen areas are family, career, finances, spiritual life, health, recreation, social life, and personal growth.

Your Wheel of Life (figure below) is a circle divided into eighths. Five dots along each line segment represents a scale of 1 to 5, with 1 being the dot farthest from the center. The center of the wheel represents balance. Total balance happens when all the dots closest to the center form a perfect circle.

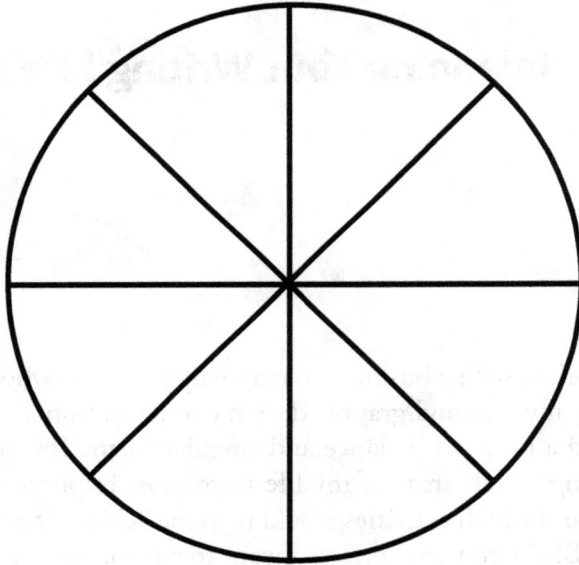

When I first did this exercise, it surprised me to see how out of balance and jagged my wheel looked. The more I performed this exercise, the better it looked and the tighter my circle became. While I never achieved a perfect circle, each week, I gained more awareness about the areas of my life that were out of balance. This constant checking in helped me to be more present and effective in each of the eight areas of my life that mattered.

As you map out your wheel, define what each segment means on your terms. For instance, if you map out fitness, what does that mean for you? If you choose spiritual life, what does that entail? Keep in mind that this exercise is your picture of success, no one else's.

What My Wheel Looks Like

Here is an example of the variables that shaped my wheel. As mentioned earlier, choose areas that matter to you and goals that make you a better, more productive person.

1. **Family.** Unplug and spend one uninterrupted hour each day with my wife and thirty minutes of uninterrupted time each day with one of my kids.
2. **Friends.** Encourage one friend daily (i.e., send a text or call, mail a card, have coffee on a weekend day).
3. **Play.** Spend thirty minutes each day doing an activity I enjoy that is unrelated to work. On the weekend, take one to two hours on a Saturday or Sunday for a self-date.
4. **Growth.** Engage in an activity for thirty minutes each day that will help me grow in any of the other seven categories.
5. **Health.** Walk or run 3-5 miles each day when workable. If outdoor activity is unavailable or unachievable due to weather, injury, or illness, perform other activities, such as yoga, stretching, or basic body weight exercises. I will also get adequate sleep (seven hours), eat balanced meals, and stay hydrated.
6. **Finances.** Be smart with money and review my family's finances daily to ensure we're always living within our means.
7. **Spiritual.** Take time to connect with God daily and invest time with others to encourage them or listen to their hearts.
8. **Career.** Create and study each day. This includes watching videos, listening to podcast, and reading 10 pages each day.

Regular practice using this will astonish you—and bring you into a good balance. It may seem difficult at first, but don't give up on it. Knowing yourself gets you comfortable in your skin.

You may wonder what this has to do with writing. I have found that when I don't have a firm grasp on my life, my writing gets muddy. I'm distracted by loose ends from external circumstances stemming from something on my wheel being out of sync. When my life is closer to the center, I am happier, the people around me are happier, and it opens valuable writing time—and my creativity isn't hijacked.

The Trivial Many and the Vital Few

The Trivial Many and the Vital Few declutters your schedule and get you focused on the most important thing—writing. When I first did this exercise, I couldn't believe how many things I let distract me in the name of "accomplishing work tasks." Many of the things on our to-do lists are time wasters and procrastination tactics designed to give the illusion of productivity (If you've ever felt accomplished after deleting email, you know what I mean). Done right, this exercise will help you eliminate those distractions, help you face your procrastination, and get you back into your writing project with renewed energy and—you guessed it—with more time to dedicate.

Best done weekly, the Trivial Many and Vital Few exercises get you running leaner by the month. In the figure below, you'll find an example chart.

Trivial Many

Activities you waste time performing each day that are important but not urgent. These can be eliminated, delegated, or reduced to allow the time you spend on them to be allocated to activities that matter most.

Activity	Current Action	New Action
Checking email	I check email every thirty minutes.	Check email three times per day (9 am, 12 pm, 3 pm).
Checking social media	I check social media every hour.	Schedule posts and designate time after working to respond.
Texting	I respond to all text messages as they arrive.	I respond to text messages after my focus work is done.

Vital Few

Activities improve your results when more time is invested in them. When you adjust the trivial many, the time saved can be invested into the activities below.

Activity	Current Action	New Action
Querying editors	I query one editor per day.	I will now query four editors per day.
Work on manuscript	I spend thirty minutes each day writing.	I will spend one hour each day writing my book.

Once you flesh out the chart, you know where you're wasting time, how much time it's costing you, and you now have a plan to solve it. You can spend the reclaimed hours writing. If you commit to using the Wheel of Life and the Trivial Many and Vital Few, you'll find balance in your life, eliminate procrastination, and open more time for writing.

Takeaways

1. The best writers are those who are self-disciplined. Creating balance and harmony in your everyday life will help you to stay in a good creative workflow.
2. Figure out what's distracting you and minimize it or get rid of it. It can be apps on your phone, social media, checking email, etc. If it's not mission critical, it's not on top of the list.

3. Check in with your lists over time to see how you're progressing. Continue to eliminate things that don't help you reach your goal. Pay attention to areas of weakness too and ask yourself if you can strengthen those areas.

Building a Brand

"A brand for a company is like a reputation for a person. You earn reputation by trying to do hard things well." - Jeff Bezos

CHAPTER 9

Designing Your Logo

If there's one lesson to learn from our image-conscious, look at me social media landscape, it's that you are the brand. Not your books—you. To create a recognizable brand, you need to know what you want to stand for. In this chapter, I'll walk you through what you need to do to create a visual representation of your brand. From typography and style to color and image, we'll cover the basics. When we're done, you'll know what you want and how to have it created.

Start With the Familiar

Who are the writers, authors, and creative brands that resonate with you? What about them moves you? When I began this process, I audited the styles of Jeff Goins, Michael Hyatt, Chris Ducker, Ryan Blair, Gary Vaynerchuk, and others. I looked at the commonality of their brands shared, whether that was choice of fonts, use of color, whether they used an image with type, or just a typographic logo. When I created my logo, I held it up next to their logos to see how it stacked up, but I was thinking long term. My vision, and yours, should be focused on becoming a contemporary of authors we admire, and our representation needed to be on that level. Though you are a self-published author, the same professional standard as traditionally published authors judges you too. Put your best foot forward.

Think for a minute about the authors who share your audience and whose brands stand out to you. Create a list of them, complete with what you like or dislike about their branding; what grabs your attention and what doesn't. If the authors you like have several similarities in style, aim not to deviate too far if you believe this is consistent with how readers view this genre. Aim then to assimilate, not differentiate. Being different for the sake of being different isn't always a winning strategy. Just visit your local bookstore and peruse book covers in your genre to see what I mean.

What Goes Into a Good Logo?

A good logo should be uncomplicated but, on the contrary, a strong representation of you as the author and brand. Avoid the overly cute, the busy, and the illegible. Stay away from fonts that can sabotage your credibility and professional image (i.e., Comic Sans, Chalk Dust, and most script fonts). The goal is for it to be recognizable and legible on a business card or a billboard. It should also look good in black and white, showing off high contrast. Most of all, your logo should reflect your personality and the personality and position of your work. Now let's talk fonts.

Choosing the Right Font

Allow me to get technical for one moment to satisfy the designers in the room. You may hear some people say font and others say typeface. Without confusing you, here is the major difference: a font exists as part of a typeface. Garamond is a typeface—it comprises a whole collection of fonts with varying weights, styles, and sizes (e.g., Garamond Regular, Garamond Bold, etc.). Think of them as little font families. When using just one iteration, say Garamond Italic, you're using a font. When using Garamond Bold as a chapter title and Garamond Regular as your paragraph copy, you're using a typeface (or family). Are you still with me?

That said, you don't have to concern yourself with it. You can call it all font and your designer will know what you mean and have no judgment (whew!). We'll refer to them all as fonts (and font families) for the rest of this chapter.

Fonts choices can make or break your logo. When designing a logo, choose between a sans serif (no little feet) and a serif (little feet on the ends) treatment. Choosing the right font for you depends on whether you are looking to be perceived as conservative, classical, modern, whimsical, or contemporary. Here are twenty fonts that cover the bases for any of those styles:

- Acre
- Alberobello Serif
- Bison
- Brandon Grotesque
- Breadley Sans
- Farnham Headline
- Galey
- Gibson
- Gilroy
- Goldplay
- Gotham
- Helvetica Neue
- Kholdby
- Madley
- Montserrat
- Sovana

- Sublima
- The Sans
- Urbine
- Welland

There are many fonts to choose. Some you pay for, others are free. I always recommend the paid fonts (many of which are included in Adobe Typekit if you have Creative Cloud). This gets you around any potential licensing issues and provides complete access to all variations of the font (i.e., bold, italic, black, ultra). If you choose a free font, be sure that all the characters, numbers, and special characters are included in that font family. I've been unpleasantly surprised to find after downloading a font that it didn't have numbers, certain forms of punctuation, or varying weights.

I mentioned avoiding script fonts. If you must use them because it reflects your personality, be sure they are legible in large and small formats. Script fonts are harder to read and don't reproduce as cleanly when reduced in size. I have known some people to brilliantly use script fonts in logos, and I have known others who have used beautifully designed hand-rendered fonts with success. Again, think about what it is you want your brand to convey in the minds of readers and begin there.

Color

Color is a major deciding factor with consumers regarding their perception of a brand and whether they will use or trust that brand. In an article in Fast Company titled, "Why Our Brains Crave Storytelling in Marketing," Rachel Gillett wrote, "According to research compiled by web design and marketing company WebPageFX, people make a subconscious judgment about a product in less than 90 seconds of viewing, and most of these people base that assessment on color alone. Almost 85% of consumers cite color as the primary reason they buy a particular product, and 80% of people believe color increases brand recognition."

In the story, Gillett broke down each color and the feelings and emotions attached to each. In summary, here's what she found:

- **Red** is a high-arousal color, often stimulating people to be bold and take risks. It stimulates the senses, raises blood pressure, and may arouse feelings of power, energy, passion, love, aggression, or danger. Red encourages impulse and drive. When used in restaurant logos, it stimulates appetite (and now you know why every fast-food restaurant has a red logo!). Brands using this color are Netflix, McDonald's, Target, and Pinterest.
- **Yellow** stimulates feelings of optimism and hope. It engages mental processes and encourages communication. In marketing, yellow is used to project youthfulness and show clarity. Brands using yellow logos include Post-It, Ikea, Snapchat, and Best Buy.
- **Blue** calms the senses and lowers blood pressure. It stimulates feelings of trust, security, order, and cleanliness. Blue increases productivity and is often preferred by men. In marketing, blue is used to signify a business as corporate. Brands cited are LinkedIn, Twitter, Facebook, and Ford.
- **Orange** stimulates feelings of energy, balance, and warmth. Orange reflects enthusiasm. In marketing, it's used to display confidence and playfulness. Brands using orange are Nickelodeon, Tinder, SoundCloud, and The Home Depot.
- **Green** relates to nature, health, good luck—and jealousy. Green stands for balance and tranquility, symbolizes money, and represents things new or growing. In marketing, you can find green used to relax consumers and put them at ease. Brands with green logos are Whole Foods, Starbucks, Spotify, and Fidelity.
- **Purple** is a low-arousal color associated with spirituality,

mystery, royalty, success, wisdom, or arrogance. In marketing, it's linked to beauty and is the hallmark of brands considered to be creative, imaginative, or wise. Brands cited are Roku, Hallmark, FedEx, and Monster.

- **Pink** signifies femininity. In marketing, the consumer feels love, warmth, sweetness, sexuality, and nurturing. Brands using pink well are Barbie, Susan G. Komen, Victoria's Secret, and Cosmopolitan.
- **Black** is formal, strong, and mysterious. The color conveys luxury, seriousness, elegance, and boldness to consumers. Brands using black logos include Apple, Louis Vuitton, Nike, Sony, Prada, and Coach.
- **Brown** relates to the nurturing traits of Mother Earth. In marketing, it conveys reliability, dependability, longevity, and support. Brands using brown are UPS, Hershey's, A&W, and M&M.

Now that you have a better understanding of type and color used in logos, let's talk about working with a designer to put it all together.

Outsourcing Design: Managing the Process

Unless you're a trained graphic designer with experience developing logos, I don't recommend tackling this yourself. Your logo is the front-facing representation of your brand. It's what people will see on your website, social media channels, and any electronic or print marketing collateral you create. That said, you want to come to any designer you contact as prepared as you can be. Here is what you'll want to do:

1. **First, do as much research as you can so that you're fully prepared.** Designers like to know they're working with a client who has some idea of what they want in their logo design. Telling your designer "I'll know what

I want when I see it" is the fastest way to frustrate a designer and increase the price of your project. Designers need your preferences for a smooth process. Have a swipe file of designs you like to share with your designer.

2. **Have a rough idea as to the fonts you wish to use.** If you do not know the names of the fonts, but can locate examples online through a Google search, then download the images to show your designer. While we're talking image search, I recommend finding logos that are similar to the look and feel you're striving to emulate. Submitting three or four different logos that match your vision will give your designer a clear idea of what you're looking to accomplish.

3. **Communicate your wishes clearly.** Let your designer know which colors you like and if you desire a text-only logo or one with an image or illustration. Also tell your designer if you plan to use a tagline within your logo or within a variation of your logo. By the same token, let them know you would like an icon-based version of the final design for social media use.

4. **Agree on the scope of work and terms.** Have a written (or electronic) agreement. In these terms, know how many versions they will design, how many revisions you'll be given once you choose a design, the studio fee for going over on revisions, whether they will deliver the complete package for that price (i.e., all native files of the logo in every print and web format) or if there is an additional fee for this service, and the turnaround time.

It will typically take up to one week for your designer to turnaround the first set of proofs for your review. I recommend you be brutally honest with your designer if you don't like your logo or want certain changes made. You will not hurt their feelings—it's their job to give you the logo that you want and paid for. This logo represents your brand. Ensure that it meets your standards matters before you request the final package.

The File Formats Your Designer Will Provide

Once your final logo is completed, you will need to get all your files from the designer. Each file format has a specific purpose. Here are the formats you'll need to request and what they're used for:

- **.tiff.** This is format supported by all aspects of print design (i.e., business cards, flyers, postcards, etc.).
- **.ai.** This is the original Adobe Illustrator file format.
- **.eps.** The gold standard in logo file formats. If nothing else, get this file from your designer. Though you may not be able to open it, your printer will ask for it. Files in this format can be enlarged and decreased in size without losing image quality.
- **.jpeg.** This is a web-based file format to be used online on websites and social media.
- **.gif and .png.** This file format allows for transparent backgrounds that are great for websites.

It's equally important to get any fonts used by your designer, copies of your logo in each of the above file formats in grayscale (black and white), and the Pantone (PMS) colors used. These colors will be useful to help you stay on brand help designers you hire to stay on brand.

Where to Find a Designer

I recommend you locate and hire a graphic designer you know, or someone recommended to you. Working on your logo with someone in your network is invaluable. You'll have a more collaborative experience and get a better understanding of the process. On the flip side, I have worked with many contractors online without issue. You can use these three websites to locate quality freelance graphic designers.

Fiverr (fiverr.com). If you need to have your logo designed with a quick turnaround time, try Fiverr (or its high-level platform Fiverr Studio). When choosing a designer on Fiverr, review their entire profile to see if their portfolio aligns with the style of design you're seeking. Design isn't one size fits all. Every designer has a style they're known for, and you can figure that out by looking at their work and the terms and conditions attached to the gig. The designer will tell you how long it takes to design the first set of logos, how many versions and revisions you'll receive, the file formats returned to you, and more. The more you need, the more it will cost.

Once you have settled on a designer, interview them via the messaging feature to fill them in on what your desired outcome is before hiring them. They all prefer you do it this way to prevent a hiring mismatch. Contractors on Fiverr are easy to work with and many of them will allow you to purchase quick turnarounds if you need your design completed rapidly (additional fees apply). I recommend Fiverr only to those who know what they want

Upwork (upwork.com) If you're looking to have more control over the design, try Upwork. With Upwork, you can shop designers much like you can Fiverr, but you'll get much more leeway for the money. Unlike Fiverr, there are no gig levels. You set the price for the work you want, write a description of the job, attach any example designs for reference, make stipulations as to who you'd prefer to work with, and list your job. Designers will match your offer, come in below your offer, or counteroffer. Review their cover letters, look at their portfolio, interview them, and then hire the best candidate. Upwork is great for those who know what they want, but it's especially helpful to those who aren't entirely sure what they want and need a little hand holding.

99designs (99designs.com) With 99designs, you choose a package that best fits your budget and then you turn it over to a group of crowdsourced designers as part of a design contest. Many people like this option as it gives more options and variations from designers competing for your business. It's a bit more expensive, but you have many hands working at once on your logo, which is helpful to some people who may want to see iterations of their logo in real-time before identifying a designer. Once you receive the designs back, you choose the design you like, and that designer works with you to create your final logo.

Logo design is a process. Take your time and think about what you want your brand to convey. Be deliberate with your type choice, your color scheme, and imagery, and who and how you have it designed. This is the most important aspect of presenting your writing business to the world. And remember, we all compete with the J.K. Rowlings, James Pattersons, Brene Browns, and Ryan Holidays of the industry. Look the part.

Takeaways

1. Designing a logo establishes you as a brand, not just as an author. It builds trust and shows commitment and longevity.

2. Be hands on and deliberate about choosing fonts and colors. Too conservative and you get lost; too "out there" and you won't be taken seriously.

3. Be well prepared before you hire a designer. It will make their job easier and ensure you get something close to what's in your mind's eye the first time. Don't make them guess.

4. You're competing with traditionally published authors. Don't forget that. Your audience demands the same level of professionalism—they deserve it.

CHAPTER 10

Creating Your Business Card

Though we're deep into the digital age, business cards prove to be a value leave behind for authors. Your business card needs to be an accurate representation of you as an author while offering your potential readers a way to contact you and access your website and social media. Let's dive in to see what works best to turn heads on this still valuable marketing tool.

What Goes on Your Card?

Business cards are essential for networking, book festivals, general promotion, and speaking events. When designing your business card, here's information to include:

- Your name
- Your phone number (optional)
- Your email address
- Your logo
- Your tagline

- Your website URL
- Social media icons
- Where your books can be found

You don't need all of these points of access, but choose the ones that direct the reader to the places you want them to connect with you.

Sizes and Styles

I recommend you use the standard 3 ½-inch by 2-inch business card. There can be a lot of printing creativity you can incorporate into this format. Whether it's a Lux card (a heavy card with accent-colored edges), a spot UV finished card (matte card with a high gloss over your logo), or a letterpress card (imprinted text), a standard card can be a billboard highlighting your creative range. Be sure to think of ways you can use color, too. Can you color the entire back of the card? Can you accent color parts of your card? Will color make important text stand out? Once upon a time, double-sided cards were expensive, nowadays online printers offer a small fee—and sometimes no fee at all—for two-sided printing. It's something I encourage you to try. In doing so, you can develop a high-quality business card on a limited budget by using a good design.

Here are a few tips for creating a business card that gets noticed:

- **Use both sides of your card.** You won't regret it, and it shows that you have invested money into your business. And if it costs little or no extra and it makes sense for you, why not?
- **Be smart with fonts.** One temptation to be aware of is using unrelated fonts on your business card. An unrelated font is any font that is not associated with your

brand. When deciding on your logo, you—or you and your designer—should select the font or font family that represent your brand. Once chosen, additional fonts on marketing collateral should be avoided or used strategically. With font families (like Helvetica, Gotham, etc.), use a weighted variation (i.e., Medium, Bold, or Black) to highlight important information. Experiment with color, using primary or accent color from your logo.

- **Go heavy on the stock.** I like weightier stock on business cards because it leaves an impression and feels higher quality. Aim for 14-point or 16-point stock. Rectangular cards are standard, but you can choose rounded corners, square cards, and smaller rectangular cards.
- **Choose the right stock for your brand.** There are three standard stocks most people choose: glossy, matte, and letterpress. Let's examine each.

  - Glossy stocks are commonly seen and allow cards using color as a design element to show vibrantly. It's also a great stock for those using photography to drive their brand image on the card. The drawback of glossy stocks is the inability to write on them with anything other than a marker.
  - Matte stocks can come uncoated or with a light coating that maintains their dull finish. These stocks are good if you have a contemporary feel. Unlike glossy cards, a coating does not protect these and if you're using white stock, they can become dingy in cardholders, your purse, or pocket.
  - A textured card, like linen, has more teeth and is best used for letterpress printing. This means that your card will have the feel of the type as you run your fingers across it. I recommend these only if you're looking for a very serious or classic look.

Printing Your Cards

While I recommend allowing your designer to broker the printing for you, online printing is quick, easy, and inexpensive. Just upload the PDF file of your card and you're in business. Today, many offer premium stock and styles that would cost you hundreds of dollars ten years ago for a fraction of the price. Spending $100 then would get you 500 single-sided cards in one color if you were lucky. Now, it could put a set of impressive business cards in your hands. Here are five online printers; some I have used, others which have come highly recommended by colleagues.

- Vistaprint (vistaprint.com)
- GotPrint (gotprint.com)
- Jukebox Print (jukeboxprint.com)
- Overnight Prints (overnightprints.com)
- Moo (moo.com)

Concluding Thoughts on Business Cards

I hope you can see the value of purchasing and using business cards as part of your individual marketing. It's an inexpensive way to visibly put your contact information into the hands of another person. Here are a few more things to consider as we wrap up.

- **Order more. Save more.** When you order, start with 1,000. Printers prefer you order higher quantities as it saves them money on ink and paper output. In return for your larger order, they happily pass the savings down.
- **Reorder before you run out.** Reorder your cards once you're down to your last 100. Since it can take up to a week to get a fresh box of business cards in your hands,

stay on top of your quantity. You never want to get caught networking or at a book festival with your cards on back order. It's unprofessional and makes it appear that you don't take your work seriously.

- **Order upon changes.** If you're changing phone numbers, addresses, email addresses, websites, or anything you have listed on your card, don't strike it through with a pen or white it out. Order new cards. Recycle the old ones. Again, think professionalism. If the change can wait until you cycle through your cards or can be planned around your next order, then wait.

Now that we have the print side of your business ready to go, let's look at the digital side.

Takeaways

1. Business cards are a valuable piece of marketing for writers. Use them for networking, conferences, meet ups, and other business and book-related festivals.

2. Design your card well, but don't over-design it. If you can, hire a professional to set your cards for a professional appearance and ease of uploading for order.

3. Choose a good stock that best represents you. Many look amazing, and you can get caught up in how they look, but the thing about your brand before you buy. Does it fit the brand or clash with your style?

CHAPTER 11

Web Domain & Hosting

Your domain and website are the online representative of your brand. In choosing a domain, pick one that best reflects you professionally.

I remember when I was searching for my domain. I knew I would never find chrisjones.com, but for posterity's sake, I had to see what was available since my name would drive my brand. I scribbled on a piece of paper other variations of my name that would also keep my brand clear and recognizable. After a couple of days of experimenting with ideas, I came up with chrisjonesink. com. I chose it since ink is a nod to writing and business (a play on the abbreviation for incorporated). It fits well within my aim of helping writers grow creatively and professionally. I scrambled to godaddy.com to see if it was available and, sure enough, it was there. I purchased it immediately and locked in a few variations of it (.net, .info). My search was over, and the roller coaster of optimism, frustration, and excitement left me satisfied.

Domains 101

Domain names are inexpensive. While you can buy a domain almost anywhere, I like to use GoDaddy, where you can catch domains for as little as 99 cents for the first year on new accounts. They also do a good job of cost-cutting bundled domains, so if you want to buy all the variations, you'll save money. Some web hosting companies offer you free domains when you purchase hosting. We'll talk about hosting in the next chapter, but this is something to consider when buying domains.

Factors to Consider

Here are a few more things you'll want to consider when buying your domain:

- **Think long-term.** Purchase the domain name for the book or books in your series. This platform allows you to sell and market your book with perks, products, content, and other value for your readers. Use a single-page website or a landing page to keep it simple.
- **Keep it short.** Think about the user who will type your domain name into the address bar of their browser. One of the first domains I purchased 20 years ago was a whopping 24 characters long! It's no wonder I didn't get a lot of business. Can you imagine how long it took to type that into the address bar? Also, consider how much additional length your name will add to it when it's used as an email address or place it on a business card.
- **Don't hyphenate.** Hyphenating creates a lot of confusion when telling people the name of your website. I learned all this the hard way twenty years ago when I bought my first domain: jones-creative-solutions.com. Having a domain name that long coupled with an email address that

added five more characters, and you can see the design nightmare that can also pose on your business card and other marketing collateral.

- **Be careful of double letters.** If your name or business name has a double letter or triple letter construction, think it through. Imagine if your name was Jess Simpson. Your domain would read like this: jesssimpson.com. That's a lot of esses and a lot of room for error. Consider how you can break that up with a middle initial or combining name and industry (e.g., jsimpsonauthor.com, jessksimpson.com).

- **Watch your words.** Many years ago, someone caught Lake Tahoe tourism in a domain name nightmare that set the Internet aflame. Using Go Tahoe! as its business name, Internet users misread gotahoe.com as "Got a Hoe." Yes, the juvenile humor of the early 2000s, but the lesson remains; check your domain name for a hidden faux pas. Lake Tahoe Tourism has since changed the website address, which forwards to their present website but kept the old name as a masked forwarding address. Remember, you want to be famous, not infamous.

Now that we've rounded the bases on domains and you know what to do and what to avoid, let's examine hosting accounts. Your hosting account is what your domain and website sit on. It's like the address to your house.

Why Self-Hosting Matters

Keeping with the house analogy, let's say you wanted to build a house from the ground up. What would be your first action? If you said acquiring a plot of land, you'd be right. Once you bought your land, you'd take your architectural plans to a builder who would then erect your house. Once completed, the house would be yours to do whatever you choose.

The same principle applies in the virtual world. Just like there are owners and renters in the real world, with tax breaks and benefits that lean in favor of ownership, there are owners and renters in the virtual world with owners dictating how their content is handled and renters under the mercy of digital landlords. Let me explain.

When you purchase a hosting plan and either hire a designer to create your website or build it yourself, you're in control of 100% of your content. You choose what you share, what images you post, control your profit, can capture leads, and manage your content. In this way, you're like a homeowner with all the benefits of ownership.

When you use a free website builder like Wix, Weebly, or WordPress.com (instead of WordPress.org, which is self-hosted), you're at the mercy of the companies that provide the service. This means you're governed by the limitations of the free platform and its rules and community guidelines. The latter can lead to you being removed from the platform at their discretion.

The same is true of social media and attempting to use Facebook as a substitute for a website. I'm sure you've heard the stories of people who have been placed into Facebook jail or de-platformed altogether. Having sites other than your own as your home can come at a price if how your conduct on these platforms violates any rules.

Now that we've covered the basics of content housing and you see the benefits of self-hosting, let's examine how to start the process. I've narrowed it down to a few reputable providers that are cost-effective, provide excellent customer service, are easy to use, and give you the most benefits for your money. I encourage you to research these or any hosting provider you consider and chat with their customer service representatives to ensure you're making a confident purchase.

Top Hosting Providers

I recommend WordPress. Yes, there are a lot of others in the game, like Squarespace, Wix, and Weebly, but WordPress is the most SEO-friendly and best-supported web creation platform available. Originally designed for bloggers, the platform transitioned into content-rich websites that Google loves to crawl. There is a slight learning curve that comes with building out a WordPress website these days, but like your design work, this too can be contracted out to someone who can place your template onto your hosting account and have you up and running in no time. That said, here are three hosting providers offering complete WordPress support and setup.

- **GoDaddy** (godaddy.com). I've hosted my website with GoDaddy since 2008 and have never had a problem with the hosting or the level of customer service I've received. For the first year, you'll pay about $84 and you'll get a free SSL certificate for that year, a free domain, free email, GoDaddy Payments (great eCommerce add-on), and website backup protection with 1-click restore.
- **Bluehost** (bluehost.com). Bluehost's plans start at less than $32 for the first year. Bluehost's basic plan comes with one website, WordPress integration, free domain, and free SSL certificate.
- **HostGator** (hostgator.com). HostGator's plans start at less than $75 for the first three years. After 36 months, you'll need to renew for another three years to keep the current price. A basic plan comes with a single website, one-click WordPress installation, a free SSL certificate, and a free domain included.

There are many hosting companies out there. Who you choose is up to you. Be sure what they offer is of value to what your goals are for your writing business. I recommend you wisely choose a builder who will provide the SSL within the package. Your SSL, short for secure socket layer, provides a security protocol that ensures privacy and integrity on the web. In short, you'll get the padlock next to your domain name in the address bar showing users that they can securely visit your site and, if necessary, make transactions without fear of fraud.

A Word on Email

If we're going to discuss hosting packages, we should talk email. I won't spend a lot of time on this topic other than to say branded email is worth the cost. Your professional credibility takes a hit when you use web-based services, like Hotmail and Yahoo! as your primary working account. Gmail is the exception if you elect to use Google Workspace and host your email through Google. You then can use your domain to create branded email accounts. This low-cost option starts at $6 per month. In that package, you're also given the full battery of Google apps. It's also easy to transfer existing Google Calendar, Drive, and contacts into your new plan. Having domain-specific email is a small investment for the value it portrays. It's the difference between chrisjonesink@gmail.com and chris@chrisjonesink.com.

Once you've set up your email address, don't forget to create a signature. Your signature should have your name, your title, your business name (or logo), and contact information. Wise Stamp (wisestamp.com) is a website that allows you to create impressive email signatures. They have free and paid plans depending on your desired use. Within your signature, be sure to add links to other pertinent access points like your social media channels, your Amazon or Book Bub author page, or podcast, if you have one.

I hope you can see the value in planning domains, self-hosting your website, and using branded email. It puts a strong professional foot forward as you build and grow your author brand. Next, we'll talk about prettying up that website you're about to create.

Takeaways

1. While it's an investment, building an author platform on your own hosted domain gives you freedom and control to manage our brand and message to your liking.

2. Keep your domains short, simple, and branded as much as possible. Be mindful of double and triple letter stacking and potential misreading.

3. Get branded email. Your professional credibility matters.

CHAPTER 12

Planning Your WordPress Website

In the early days of the Internet, websites were coded by hand, and if you wanted a website built, you had to hire a web designer and sometimes a web programmer—one to create the art and the other to add the functionality. Those days are long gone, and now, you can hop online and purchase fully designed templates with baked-in functionality. You still may have to hire someone to install it and set it up for you, but the cost is minuscule compared to the old days of the Web.

WordPress themes range from open source (free) to any-where from under $10 and upwards of $80 or more. When choosing a theme, think about who you are as a brand or on what your website will focus upon. It's easy to chase cool look-ing themes only to find that 1) it's more website than you want or need, 2) it's difficult to manage with its many functions, 3) it buries your message entirely.

Many sites allow you to search for themes by industry or style. If your goal is to have a portfolio site, many templates focus on showing off your assets. If you aim to create a hub for selling your books and engaging with readers, the same is true.

Narrowing down your objectives starts the process. If you're not sure what type of website you want to have, I have an exercise for you to try right now.

Auditing for Aesthetics & Functionality

On a sheet of paper, list 5-10 author websites you like and that have functions and features you might want on your website. These features can be subscription pop-ups, social media buttons, image sliders, book portfolios with e-commerce ability, or landing pages for giveaways. Below are questions you'll want to consider as you audit these websites.

Aesthetics

- How is the home page presented and what's "above the fold" (i.e., is shown before you must scroll)?
- Is their blog on the home page or under a designated tab?
- Are the social media links prominent?
- Is it easy to subscribe to the website?
- Does the website have a visible offer?
- Are books listed on the home page? Where? How?
- Are the fonts clear and strong? How does it make the site appear? What does it say about the author?
- Are there common color themes among the sites you like?

Functionality & Engagement

- Go through the navigation. Do you like how it flow? Do the titles work? Which titles would you use?
- How much navigation do they use? Are there drop-down menus? How are those treated?
- How and where do they promote their books?
- How are the About and Contact pages written?
- Is there a media page? How is it arranged?

- Is there a call to action? On how many pages? On which pages?

As you take the time to audit author websites, note what traditionally published authors are doing with their websites and think about implementing some of the same functionality and aesthetics. Then find a template that is customizable to the level you seek, is easy enough for you to manage, and comes out of the box with tools you need (many can be added with WordPress's extensive library of plugins).

Where to Find a Theme

While there are many sites to choose from, here are my recommendations:

- ThemeForest (themeforest.net)
- Elegant Themes (elegantthemes.com)
- WooThemes (woothemes.com)
- Template Monster (templatemonster.com)

Any of those four sites provide you premium WordPress themes, and they are not expensive. TemplateMonster is my favorite. Its themes are well done, well documented, and well worth the money. They also offer template installation for a nominal fee at the point of purchase.

One other note on themes: choose a responsive template. This means when users view it from screens of varying sizes, your website will scale to fit the size of the screen, and nothing gets lost.

Getting Help

Once you've settled on a WordPress theme, you will need help installing it if you're not comfortable installing and customizing the template. Something I learned when buying themes is that some don't come out of the box looking the way you see them in the on-screen demos. They have to be built out once installed, so I recommend investing in a WordPress web designer. You can find these in your network, through friends, on Upwork or Fiverr, or Envato Studio (studio.envato.com).

I found all of my web designers online and have maintained off-site relationships with those who have done great work so I can contact them as needed. After you buy your template, supply them with files and access to your hosting account for installation. Once they design the site and get it back to you, you'll want to become familiar with the new tools you have at your fingertips. Content management sites, like WordPress, have made it easy for even those who profess to have little technological prowess, as you'll see in the next chapter.

Takeaways

1. Study the site strategy of traditionally published authors. In the words of Bruce Lee, "Absorb what is useful. Discard what is not. Add what is uniquely your own."

2. When creating your website, aim to be more professional than pretty. It will do you no good to have the best-looking site if you can't update it yourself (and if users can't navigate it easily).

3. Hire a WordPress web designer to help you set your website up, add the functionality you want, and teach you how to use it.

CHAPTER 13

WordPress Dashboard Basics

Now that you've locked in your domain and hosting, selected your template, and had it installed onto your WordPress website, it's time to become familiar with what's under the hood. This chapter serves as more of a primer than an in-depth guide since there are many videos covering WordPress basics on YouTube. I'll list a few at the end of this chapter.

When you log into the admin panel of your WordPress website (yoursitename.com/wp-admin), you'll see your dashboard. Here's what you'll find:

- **Updates.** This area lets you know when your plugins or themes have new updates. Out of the box, you won't have any necessary updates, but monitor this area. When plugins aren't updated, they can cease to function and can sometimes cause other plugins to not work at all. When you click on the link, you'll land on a page showing which items need updating. Tick the Select All box and then click Update Plugins.

- **Posts.** This area houses your blog posts. To understand the relationship between a page and a post in Word-Press, think of your WordPress site as a filing cabinet. Pages are the folders and posts are the documents within the folders. The label you stick on the folder is your navigational tab. Each post represents a new article on your website. Be sure to give your post an optimized name and a brief description that Google can search, rank, and index. I recommend you install the Yoast SEO plugin. It makes optimizing your posts for Google simple and effective, providing you a red, yellow, and green coding system to help you improve your SEO.
- **Categories and Tags.** You'll find these menu options when hover over Posts. Categories allow you to index your posts topically if you want to create separate menus for each category you cover on your website. For example, you could have a navigational drop-down tab called Services and within that menu would be a sub-menu for each service you provide. The pages behind each sub-menu are driven by your Categories designations. Tags allow you to inform users of the varying subjects they can expect to find within the post. If you created a post on how to start a podcast, your tags might be podcast equipment, podcasting, Adobe Audition, Audacity, iTunes, etc.
- **Media.** True to its name, the media section stores your visual files. When you upload a new picture, image, document, or video, take the time to optimize it by giving a meaningful name that Google can categorize (image.jpg does not work!) and that defines what's in the image, document, or video. Use the alt name to describe the image. This helps the visually impaired who use interpretation software to "read" the image. Then add a keyworded description. These few extra seconds of doing your due diligence will pay off long term. One thing to note—make sure you size your images for your website. If your

post's featured image renders at 800 pixels by 600 pixels, make sure your image is exactly those dimensions. Yes, WordPress will resize it for you, but at the cost of page load speed.

- **Pages.** Pages control the static elements on your website, those pages involving few or minor content changes over time like your Contact or About page. Pages are where you'll base much of your navigation. Your Home, About, Services, Books, Contact, or other pages you develop for your website stem from this section.

- **Comments.** You'll see a number pop up from this section when new comments hit your blog. When you click on it, you'll see the comments and can accept the comments, reply to them, or designate them as spam and discard them. If you want to moderate your comments, which I recommend, click on the Settings tab, and under Discussions, check the box "Comment must be manually approved" next to the "Before a comment appears" subheading. Look at the complete discussions page for other ways to manage comments. To best manage comments, I recommend installing the Disqus plugin. It allows Disqus users easier sign-in access to your website to leave comments. I also find it easier to moderate.

- **Appearances.** In the Appearance tab, you'll find all your theme settings and your menus. This is where you will build out your website or change your website. The Appearance tab allows you to go into the theme and update it as you see fit. You can change some themes by pointing and clicking on options. For instance, you can add your social media links, change the website title, upload a new logo and a favicon, and experiment with color. It affects nothing, and no coding is required. You can also change the style sheets here too. If you're unfamiliar with CSS style sheets, this won't pertain to you, and I recommend you ask your web designer for those changes (usually about font styles and elements you want to remove that are hard coded into the website template).

- **Widgets.** Widgets are plugins you can use to add more visual content to your website. Most widgets appear in the sidebar of your website. Think about some websites you have seen that have Twitter feeds, related posts, offers, or ads on the side of the screen. Those run by widgets. Some advanced widgets cost money while others are free. Some offer free versions with basic functionality and add-ons for a small price to give you more power.
- **Menus.** This section is where you'll create a structured navigational menu. Choose the Pages, Categories, or tags you want to be featured in your navigation, and then click Add to Menu. Drag and drop them into any order that suits you. You can create drop-down menus by nesting the tabs you create below one another. If you want to link outside of your website, for instance, to your Amazon profile or your Goodreads page, choose Custom Links and insert the link. If you want to create a navigational tab that goes nowhere but that houses a drop-down to other menu items, choose Custom Links and insert a hashtag (#) in place of the URL. This tells the website that this page goes nowhere, and visitors won't be able to click through it.
- **Screen Options.** At the top right of the page is a menu option called Screen Options. Click the tab and when it opens, check the Link Target box. This will enable each menu item you create to have an extra step within it to give you control of outbound content. If you want to send users out of your website, checking the now-visible "Open link in a new tab" option in the menu tab allows you to send users to those outside pages through a new browser tab. This keeps users on your site. Good web practice is you always want to keep users on your website and if you send them out, send them through a new tab.
- **Plugins.** Plug-ins add all the bells and whistles to your website. There are plugins for optimization, for adver-

tising, for social media, for podcast audio, for video, for selling products, for signing up visitors, for email newsletters or other subscription-based services, and the list goes on. If you see a number displayed, it signals you need to update a plugin.

Here are a few I recommend:

- **Askimet.** This plugin controls comment spam should you use the native WordPress comments. It's $5, but it filters tons of spam.
- **Yoast SEO.** This is the best SEO plugin I've used. It's user friendly and creates your sitemap, grades your optimization, and allows you to customize your post descriptions for social media sharing. This is the key benefit to making sure your website has a chance of being noticed by Google.
- **Contact Form 7.** It's a simple contact form. If you want a more robust form, try Gravity Forms. It sells for $40 and offers more detailed user data capture options.
- **W3 Total Cache.** This plugin caches your website to ensure peak performance and download speed.
- Better Delete Revisions. WordPress keeps files of every post update you make. This plugin clears those out, so those redundant files don't affect site speed.
- **Really Simple Captcha.** If you want to ensure users completing your web forms aren't robots, this creates a captcha code that asks users to translate words or do the math before submitting.
- **WordPress to Dropbox.** This plugin sends a backup of your website to your Dropbox account, so if something goes wrong with your website, you always have a recent backup to import. Use this in tandem with your hosting provider's backups.
- **Users.** This section allows you to add contributors to

your website. If you plan to have guest postings, you can add new authors here. There is a free plugin called WP Users that allows you to add social media links to each user's profile on your website. Most themes come with the ability to have authorship pulled from a Word-Press-owned site called Gravatar (gravitar.com). Complete your profile there, and you can use your author avatar anywhere.

- **Tools.** If you plan to import content from another installation of WordPress or if you want to move your site to another hosting provider by exporting it, this is where you'll do it. This involves basic technical know-how, so consult your programmer before you attempt to use this option.
- **Settings.** Your settings section is where you can change time zones, dates, the website title, how the URL appears in Google, designate an email address for post comments and for forms to write back to, and more. Spend a little time looking over each of the options to see how they apply to your site.

Getting More Familiar

If you want to learn more about the WordPress dashboard and see the functions in real-time, check out these demonstrational videos. I've also included a pair of videos on Yoast SEO. I can't stress proper base-level optimization enough.

- **WordPress Walkthrough Series (by BlueHost):** rebrand.ly/WP-Made-Easy
- **How To Make a WordPress Website - 2018 - In 24 Easy Steps:** rebrand.ly/WP-TylerMoore
- **Yoast SEO Free:** rebrand.ly/Yoast-SEO-Basic
- **WordPress SEO Tutorial for Beginners:** rebrand.ly/SEO-Ahrefs

This chapter is a quick and dirty tour of the WordPress environment. It's an easy platform for the most basic user. As you become more and more acclimated to it, you'll find you made the right choice, and you'll be able to use its scalability to monetize it.

Takeaways

1. WordPress is a content management system used to run your website. Taking the time to learn how to navigate your website will make updating it easier for you (and saves you time and money long term).

2. Understanding how to set up WordPress from the admin end and add basic SEO on your website will go a long way to helping your author brand rank on Google.

Promote Your Brand

"People do not buy goods and services. They buy relations, stories and magic." – Seth Godin

CHAPTER 14

Tips for Social Media Engagement on Facebook, Twitter and LinkedIn

I hosted a children's book author on my podcast a few years ago. During the interview, I asked her what the one thing was that no one tells you about self-publishing. Without hesitation, she said the hard work that comes after you've published your book. You have to think, act, and work like a publisher. And she's right. I've asked this question in many interviews, and the answer is nearly always the same—promoting is the hardest work.

It takes grit and hustle to sell your work. We believe once we publish on Amazon, everyone will show up waiting to whip out their credit cards and buy our books. That's not the case. Until we make it known that our book is available, it will sit on Amazon, taking up space and falling in rank. Sure, someone may stumble upon it and purchase it, but that's the exception and not the rule. If we want to sell books, we need to open our mouths or publish content on social media.

Building a Social Community

If you're on social media, you're already part of the community. The next step is investing in it for the benefit of growing your presence. In his best-selling book, *The 7 Habits of Highly Effective People*, Dr. Stephen F. Covey said nothing in creation can escape what he coins as The Law of the Farm. On a farm, there is a season for everything—preparing the fields, planting the seeds, watering the fields, allowing nature to nurture, harvesting, and then enjoying the fruits of your labor. The same is true of building your online community. It's a slow-growing and intentional process. Be patient and work at it consistently to see maximum benefit. Here are a few tips I've learned over the years to help you develop and cultivate relationships online. Use what works best for you.

Facebook

Facebook has become a three-front battlefield for attention in recent years. From its initial offering of personal profiles, the platform has expanded to offer business pages and groups. Each facet of the service requires its own strategy. Here are some recommended ways to use Facebook to increase your audience and grow your social capital.

Personal Page. Use your page to maintain connections within the general Facebook population. You'll find that most of your connections will engage on your page more often than they do on your business page. I recommend using your page like you would your business page and even in tandem. On your page, openly talk about your work, promote your books, share your life behind the scenes, post your reviews. Here are other ways to get the most from your page:

- Create a cover image to promote your book. Get this done on Fiverr or Upwork for a few bucks to ensure it looks strong and engaging.
- Use the Bio to tell friends and followers what you write and how to get your book.
- Use the photo grid area as free advertising. Create one promotional graphic and drop it in there with a link in the caption to how to take advantage of it.
- Make any relevant work experience visible and link it to your author page.
- Record Facebook Live videos and talk about your book, share interesting aspects of your writing life, broadcast from conferences and festivals, and host AMAs (Ask Me Anything) to let friends and followers pick your brain. You can even do unboxing videos when new books arrive and make pre-launch or launch announcements.
- Poll your friends. When you need research for a book, help to choose a book title or a cover, or some other aspect related to your work, put it out there and get some engagement. I have had author clients show off their cover concepts so their friends can vote to choose the best cover.
- When you have speaking engagements, book signings, or other events, create a Facebook Event and place it on your wall. Be sure to invite people to attend once you do.
- Use the Life Events tab to document book releases, conferences attended, speaking engagements, and other important career or life events.
- Have fun. Facebook can be a place where politics and social justice can bring out the best or worst in people. Keep it light and stay positive, and you'll enjoy engaging your audience.

Business Page. Business pages give you additional tools personal pages lack, like the ability to create ads, boost posts, cross-promote advertising with Instagram, create offers, and more. Facebook has caught a lot of criticism for its suppression of business pages, particularly with local businesses. The network has altered its algorithms in ways that make pages difficult to see in user timelines (unless you're a paid advertiser to which Facebook then gives you some leverage). Despite it all, having a business page is still a good idea. Positioned right, you can make it into a public relations extension of your website by giving it similar branding, flow, and feel. Here are ways to get the most out of business pages:

- Create a cover photo that defines the page. My cover is a replica of my website header. Yours can be the same, or it can promote a current book or book series.
- Complete every section of the profile. The more information you provide, the easier it is for users to contact you.
- Encourage user reviews. If you have followers who love talking about your books or enjoy working with you, ask them for a review. Remember, people make buying decisions based on social media recommendations.
- Keep a running calendar in your events section. Let your followers know what sort of events you're participating in and how to find you.
- Use the video section to share podcasts or broadcast interviews you've been on, create themed playlists, and more.
- Use the Photos area to create themed albums. Facebook users love behind-the-scenes images. Create various albums for the different facets of your writing business.
- Under the Groups tab, users can find your group (or

groups). Facebook allows you to create custom invite buttons for ease of access.

- You can customize the button beneath your cover photo with preset options. Choose the one that posts regularly. While you may not get a ton of engagement initially, staying the course pays off. Ask followers to click the "Following" button next to the "Like" button and select "See First" in their news feed and turn notifications on.
- Since business pages have their own messaging system, be aggressive about responding. When you respond to messages, Facebook gives you a label based on how quickly you respond. Aim for the green "Very Responsive" designation.
- When you create posts, use the pre-set engagement options like polls and business markers like Milestones. Also, aim to be visual within your posts. Share your blog content, graphics, photos, and other images.

Groups

Facebook Groups are one of Facebook's best engagement tools. With a group page, you can create a group theme and engage a warm audience as often as you wish. I've known authors who have created groups for their readers, for books, and about book publishing tips and tactics. Unlike business pages, group members receive notifications organically. Other ways to get the most from your group:

- Create a cover image that reflects the group's theme.
- Purchase a domain for your group and forward it to your Facebook URL. This makes sharing your group easier outside of Facebook. It's easier to invite people to join your group at www.AuthorsGroup.com as opposed to www.facebook.com/groups/781495321956931/?-

multi_permalinks=1711048382354952&notif_
id=1546135954580517&notif_t=group_highlights

- Lay down your group rules in the description. If you plan to be active, a fun way to keep daily engagement is by using theme days. These are designated themes for each day of the week (e.g., Motivated Monday, Marketing Tips Tuesday, Promotion Wednesday, etc.). I've learned that members enjoy these since it's geared toward getting people to talk about themselves. In the Appendix, I've placed example rules from Facebook groups for you to model.

- If you choose the daily theme approach, have the artwork for each day's theme. I recommend using a subscription-based social media publisher, like Buffer, to schedule your releases each day. Hop in on Sunday and schedule the entire week. Be sure to have the posts publish at the same time each day so members know when to expect them.

- Place freebies and other perks in the Files section. If you have a free PDF eBook, checklist, or some other downloadable perk, stick it in files and allow the members of the group to enjoy benefits specifically for them.

- Use live streams to speak to your group, host webinars within your group, or share news.

- Set the privacy to closed. If you leave it open, anyone can join and that's not a good thing. You want to vet those who request access to protect your group from spammers. You can even set entrance interview questions that interested prospective members must first answer before consideration.

Facebook gives you the opportunity for maximum engagement if you do it well. It takes time to grow, but if you're deliberate about connecting with others, you'll see results.

Twitter

Most people I talk to say they don't get Twitter. "What's the point?" they ask. If you're looking to connect with publishers, agents, and publishing industry insiders, Twitter is where you need to be. Within the confines of Twitter, you can find agents looking for authors (on Episode 69 of my podcast, Hannah Carmack recounted how a tweet landed her a book deal), what type of manuscripts publishers are looking for, and for freelance writers, editors galore.

In case you don't know, Twitter is comprised of short messages called "tweets" limited to 280 characters. It also runs on a categorization system of hashtags. Finding the right hashtags for your industry can unlock a plethora of contacts for you.

Twitter is also about exchanging ideas, information, and engaging in conversation. Those with content to share or who become adept at "retweeting"—resharing other people's content—have productive experiences with Twitter. Here are some additional tips for making Twitter worth your time.

- Network with those in your genre. Connect with others who write in your genre, editors, publishers, and agents within their following and followers list. You can also keep pace with the news and trends they share.
- Find and follow relevant hashtags. You'll discover these as you follow editors, authors, agents, and publishers.
- Take part in Twitter chats. Seek genre-specific chats (#WomensFiction), community chats (#WritingCommunity), interest-specific chats (#BookLovers) to meet other users and discuss ideas.
- If you're looking to cozy up with magazine editors, be sure to retweet their posts and mention something you learned or liked about their article.
- Use Twitter to locate publishing partners like book editors, proofreaders, illustrators, publicists and marketers,

bookstores, and associations.

- Have fun. Engage on Twitter with everyone, from high-profile people to everyday users. You don't know where the right tweet at the right time may take you. Chacho Valdez earned his dream job at venture capitalist firm Backstage Capital when he tweeted this simple question to company founder Arlan Hamilton: "What books would you most recommend to an aspiring VC?" After some Twitter exchanges over time, Hamilton offered Valdez his dream job working for the firm.

While Twitter may not come naturally to you, learn to maximize the power of those 280 characters, and those little bursts can change your life.

LinkedIn

Dubbed the world's largest professional network, LinkedIn boasts large concentrations of professionals globally—over 500 million—and allows users to engage in online professional networking. Here are ways to get the most out of this platform:

- Use a professional photo. Unlike Facebook, which was built for personal communication, LinkedIn represents you as a brand. Put your best face forward.
- Aim to optimize your headline. While using the obvious works (i.e., CEO of Writing Words Company), using a headline focusing on the results you provide helps users to know what you do instead of where you do it. One of my clients, Marc Mawhinney, uses this headline: "I help coaches get more clients (WITHOUT paid advertising)." Can you see how that helps you now? Makes you curious to know how he does it.
- When making a connection request, always tell people

how you found them and why you want to connect. People on LinkedIn guard their network more than other platforms. Explaining why you want to connect is beneficial.

- Fill out your profile completely. Leave nothing blank where you can add meaningful information and content.
- Write your profile in first person using the reverse PAR method of writing. The PAR stands for Problem, Action, Result. Open your profile with a strong lead paragraph about yourself and your business, then share how you achieve results, which actions you take to achieve them, and which problems you solve for your clients.
- Repost past content or share new content. LinkedIn's platform is well-optimized and by sharing your content, you can reach more people, bring eyeballs back onto your website, and who knows, perhaps you can become a LinkedIn Influencer.
- Recommend people you know, like, and trust. Social capital goes a long way. Make it a habit to write recommendations to people in your network.

Ready to give a few of these tips a try on your social networks? Combined with face-to-face networking, social media is a great way to extend your reach and grow your audience.

Takeaways

1. Social media is a great way to find new readers and show people where you and your book can be found at any time. One of the key things to remember is choosing the platforms that best serve you. Not everyone best benefits you, so find out where your readers are and go there and forget the rest. Master the easy opportunities first.

2. Use social media to network and meet new people, show off your personality, and introduce people to you and your books. It's one thing to ask people to buy; it's another to sell yourself first, thus warming up the sale.

CHAPTER 15

Building Your Press Kit

You've seen author interviews on television, walked into book signings at your local bookstore, or have listened to writer interviews on your favorite podcasts, which may have left you to wonder, "How did they do that?"

With a press kit. A press kit is a package of promotional materials you can use to send to bloggers, podcast and television show hosts, bookstore marketing managers, and journalists who may be interested in reporting about you and your book. You can organize it electronically and house it on your website, or it can be a physical packet you can mail to someone who requests information about you.

If you want to nail those interviews by impressing show hosts, you'll want to make sure your press kit is top notch.

What Goes Inside Your Press Kit?

Your press kit is the most important promotional product after your book cover, which should be lights out since it's the first thing potential readers and interested media will see. Within your press kit, have these items:

- **Press release.** A press release is a brief news story you write (or have written by a public relation or communications professional) that's sent to members of the media where you best resonate and have the greatest odds being picked up. The goal of a press release is to capture interest. Your press release should answer the 5 Ws and the H (Who? What? Where? When? Why? And how?) to help the journalist, blogger, or show producer determine whether your book and its surrounding story can drive audience interest. If you only do one thing on this list, write your press release. It's the most important promotional communication for your book. I've included a sample press release in the Appendix.
- **Endorsements or recommendations.** If you haven't included these within your book, you can gather some endorsement letters showing you're a subject matter expert about the topic within your book or are a worthy speaker to consider. Use these to pitch meeting planners for booking conference speaking gigs, keynotes, and other presentations. If you don't have references, ask for them. You can also check with people in your LinkedIn network who have recommended you. Have them write a recommendation on letterhead or send you an electronic version. Treat these the way you would treat a testimonial.
- **Pitch Letter.** Write a pitch letter to the specific person you are addressing outlining who you are, what your credentials are, the value you add to their audience, and how you intend to share the interview once it goes live (i.e., Your social media networks, in your email newsletter, on your podcast, etc.). Be sure to have a level of familiarity with the person to whom you're pitching. The more you can personalize the pitch, the better. Mention

recent stories you've read by them, podcast episodes or broadcasts you've watched featuring them, and what you learned from those. Editors (and show producers) are people, too.

- **Photos.** Include a professionally shot photograph of yourself and a cover image of your book.
- **Past Press.** Be sure to have a page that includes links to past press you've received. Format should be: Title of the story, publication, publication date. (e.g., Local Author Pens Book on Space Flight Experience; *The News Daily*, Jan. 17, 2018)
- **Your Book.** For public speaking inquiries, include a copy of your book. This gives you an advantage with meeting planners who receive hundreds of pitches. Having a book allows you to stand out and adds value to positions you as a subject matter expert. If you want to go the extra mile, be sure to flag sections of particular interest within your book to the intended recipient with a brief reason why it's pertinent to their event and how you can discuss this from the stage.
- **Reviews.** If your book has received great reviews from bloggers, on Amazon or the book distributor websites, or in magazines, include those within your press kit. I had a book I co-authored reviewed by *Publisher's Weekly*, which I placed on my website and in my kit afterward. Every bit of attention you receive is worth noting.
- **Speaker bio/one sheeter (separate document).** Create a basic speaker bio/one sheeter that includes your bio, a photo, information about your book, relevant websites for accessing you and your book, your social media links, and questions for the interviewer to ask you to make for a better interview. These are invaluable to podcast and radio show hosts. When pitching them, they only require your pitch letter, speaker bio/one sheeter, photo, and book cover image.

Anatomy of a Press Release

Since a press release is the flagship marketing piece of the press kit, let's look at the anatomy of a press release so you can get an overview and a quick idea of how to write a press release.

- **Contact Information.** This sits in the upper left corner and should include on separate, single-spaced lines: your name, your company (if applicable), your phone number, your email address, and who the point of contact is if it's not you (this could be your manager or publicist).
- **For Immediate Release.** This rests in the upper right corner and lets the recipient know the press release is ready for immediate distribution. It should be bold and in all caps.
- **Headline.** Your headline needs to grab the recipient's attention right away. Don't make it too cute, too wordy, or too vague, or the opposite can happen. It should be bold and set at 14 or 18 points in a standard font (Times New Roman or Garamond). When considering your headline, think about what within your book resonates with the public or is newsworthy. If your book is about demystifying dog breeds labeled as aggressive by the public, then your headline might be: "Are Pit Bull Terriers Friendlier Than We Once Thought?" Or "New Book Explores Reasons for Aggression in Dogs (And It's Not What You Think!)." A compelling headline leads the editor inside the press release for more information.
- **Sub-headline.** Once the headline feels attractive, add a sub-headline offering more detail. Using the aggressive dog example, you could say: "New book sheds light on how training and diet affect temperament in so-called aggressive dogs" or "New book reveals training secrets of top dog trainers to help tame your dog in 90 days." Do you see how a strong headline and a good sub-headline

can draw an editor into reading the rest of your press release? Use the same font as the headline, italicize it, and
set it 2-point sizes smaller than your headline size.
- **Dateline.** On the first line with the opening sentence,
lead with a dateline. In this section, place your city and
state. Use postal abbreviations for your state (e.g., Chica-
go, IL; Glendale, AZ). Follow this with an em dash.
- **Body.** The body should read like a standard news story, as
mentioned earlier in the chapter.
- **Boilerplate.** The boilerplate is a 50-100 word "About the
Author." You can use what you use on your website or
custom fit this for the release. Place it below the body.
- **Book Information.** Add information about your book for
the recipient. Include the following in a single line of text:

  - Book title
  - Author's name
  - Release date
  - Paperback ISBN
  - Page count
  - Publisher
  - Where it's available for purchase

Once you've built your press kit, the hard part is out of the
way and all you have to do is maintain it. I recommend housing
a copy on your website under your Press page to make it easy to
share when needed.

Takeaways

1. A well-developed press kit can help you secure valuable
publicity necessary for marketing you and your book.

2. Be sure to take your time and build a strong, professional press kit. Beyond your website, your press kit will help to position you and present you with needed media opportunities.

3. Don't focus your pitch letter on who you are. Focus on who you're pitching. Remember that your recipients are looking for the next newsworthy story, the next great interview to share with their audience. It can be you if you do it right.

4. Use the one-sheeter for podcast hosts. They typically won't read a press release, but instead will skim your query email and look at your one-sheeter to see if you're a fit.

Conclusion

You made it. As you can see, we started and ended the book with confidently putting your best foot forward. Your attitude, aptitude, and focus all will determine how far you'll go in this business. To be successful as a writer, you have to be more cerebral about the processes and less romantic. While breaking into professional writing can be tough, you now have the tools to get yourself off the ground.

Cheers to a long and successful writing career!

APPENDIX A

Sharpening the Saw

Information comes to those who look for it. There is a Chinese proverb that states, "When the student is ready, the master appears." This has always been a truth in my life. When I was ready for the next level of learning, there stood the tools I needed to get me there.

These are some of the best resources I have used or that have come recommended.

Books

When I was a 21-year-old student at the Art Institute of Pittsburgh, my Adobe Illustrator professor, Dana Ingham, stopped our class one day. He reminded us of how much we were paying for our education and told us if there was anything we wanted to learn, we could find it in a book. I took that to heart and have since applied it every day of my life. Here are some influential books to get you started.

Writing & Creativity

- *The Elements of Style* by William Strunk Jr. and E.B. White
- *On Writing Well* by William Zinsser
- *On Writing* by Stephen King
- *Clarity: Towards Style & Grace* by Joseph M. Williams
- *Write, Publish, Repeat* by Sean Platt and Johnny B. Truant
- *Bird by Bird* by Anne Lamott
- *Writer to Writer* by Cecil Murphey
- *Big Magic* by Elizabeth Gilbert
- *The Artist's Way* by Julia Cameron

Business & Leadership

- *Crush It* by Gary Vaynerchuk
- *The E-Myth Revisited* by Michael Gerber
- *The 4-Hour Work Week* by Tim Ferriss
- *The Go-Giver* by Bob Burg & John David Mann
- *The 21 Irrefutable Laws of Leadership* by John C. Maxwell
- *Today Matters* by John C. Maxwell

Mentality & Work

- *Finish: Give Yourself the Gift of Done* by John Acuff
- *The Perennial Seller* by Ryan Holiday
- *The 5 Second Rule* by Mel Robbins
- *The Power of Habit* by Charles Duhigg
- *Mastery* by Robert Greene
- *Choose Yourself* by James Altucher
- *Deep Work* by Cal Newport
- *The War of Art* by Steven Pressfield
- *Breaking the Habit of Being Yourself* by Joe Dispenza
- *The New Psycho-Cybernetics* by Dr. Maxwell Maltz

Podcasts

Podcasts are easy to access, and you can learn about many topics that suit your writing and business interests. Podcasts I recommend are:

Writing & Creative Business

- *Hey, Creator*
- *The Creative Penn Podcast*
- *Book Launch Blueprint*
- *The Self-Publishing Show*
- *The Art & Business of Writing (yes, shameless plug!)*

Business & Entrepreneurship

- *Kate's Take*
- *Smart Passive Income with Pat Flynn*
- *The School of Greatness with Lewis Howes*
- *The Ed Mylett Show*
- *The James Altucher Show*
- *The Boss Mom Podcast*
- *Deep Questions with Cal Newport*

Marketing & Sales

- *Online Marketing Made Easy with Amy Porterfield*
- *The Social Media Examiner's Show*
- *The Marie Forleo Podcast*
- *Sell More Books Show*

YouTube

YouTube videos can also be a fast and free way to learn. I prefer YouTube for watching videos by leading sales influencers, motivational speakers, and lifestyle entrepreneurs. Here are a few I recommend:

- Dan Lok
- Sam Ovens
- Matt D'Avella
- Eric Thomas
- Sunny Lenarduzzi
- Thomas Frank
- Evan Carmichael

Websites/Blogs

Blogs and websites targeted at your interests and expertise are a great way to learn. Here are some of the best websites for sharpening your business acumen.

- **Entrepreneur** (entrepreneur.com). Learn how to start, run and organize your business, plus get expert tips on finance, marketing, and leadership.
- **Ragan Communications** (ragan.com). Learn to become a more effective communicator with Ragan.com. Learn about grammar, writing, press and PR tips, and get other communication advice.
- **Social Media Examiner** (socialmediaexaminer. com). Michael Stelzner developed Social Media Examiner to help businesses extend their reach through social media. The weekly newsletter coupled with the website, podcasts, and YouTube channel will prove to be an invaluable resource if you're getting started with or expanding your social media presence.

- **Publisher's Weekly** (publishersweekly.com). Get insider tips about the publishing industry, agents, and more.
- **Writer's Digest** (writersdigest.com). Written to help writers navigate every facet of their creative and professional lives, WD is a staple in the writing community.
- **Writing Routines** (writingroutines.com). Q&As from authors on their writing rituals and processes.

Writers Associations

If you want to connect with other writers for inspiration, advice, networking, and professional development, here is a listing of associations for practically every genre of writer:

- Academy of American Poets
- African American Online Writers Guild
- American Business Media
- American Christian Fiction Writers
- American Christian Romance Writers
- American Christian Writers Association
- American Copy Editors Society
- American Crime Writers League
- American Grant Writers Association
- American Medical Writers Association
- American Society of Journalists and Authors
- American Writers and Artists Inc.
- Asian American Journalists Association
- Association for Business Communication
- Association of Christian Writers

- Association of Food Journalists
- Association of Writers and Writing Programs
- Association of Young Journalists and Authors
- Authors and Publishers Association
- Authors Guild
- Black Writers Alliance
- Christian Writers Guild
- Educational Writers Association
- Erotica Readers and Writers Association
- Garden Writers Association of America
- Horror Writers Association
- Investigative Reporters and Editors
- Midwest Writers
- Military Writers Society of America
- Mystery Writers of America
- National Association of Independent Writers and Editors
- National Association of Science Writers
- National Association of Women Writers
- National Conference of Editorial Writers
- National Resume Writers Association
- National Society of Newspaper Columnists
- National Writers Association
- Native American Journalists Association
- New England Writers
- North American Travel Journalists Association
- Outdoor Writers Association of America
- Outdoor Writers Guild
- Pacific Northwest Writers Association
- Poetry Society of America
- Professional Copywriters Association
- Professional Writers Alliance
- Romance Writers of America
- Science Fiction and Fantasy Writers Association
- Science Fiction Writers of America
- Science Fiction Poetry Association

- Society of American Travel Writers
- Society of Children's Book Writers and Illustrators
- Society of Environmental Journalists
- Society of Professional Journalists
- Society of Southwestern Authors
- Southeastern Outdoor Press Association
- Southeastern Writers Association
- Technical Writers Association
- The Authors Guild
- Western Writers of America
- Women's Fiction Writers Association

APPENDIX C

Sample Press Release

Here's my press release for the book you're holding.

Media Contact Information
Chris Jones
(123) 456-7890
chris@chrisjonesink.com

** FOR IMMEDIATE RELEASE **

THE ART & BUSINESS OF WRITING IS A BOOK FOR THOSE WHO WANT TO START WRITING, AND A MARKETING GUIDE FOR THOSE WHO ALREADY DO

WILLIAMSBURG, VA—December 28, 2015—Most people have thought about writing a book in their lives. The challenge lies in where and how to start such an endeavor. Chris

Jones' book, *The Art & Business of Writing: A Practical Guide to the Writing Life*, teaches new writers where to begin without leaving experienced writers behind.

"I wrote *The Art & Business of Writing* because I believe everyone has a story that they want to share. I used my story as someone coming from an art background into writing to illustrate that anyone with a passion for writing and a willingness to persevere can do it," says Jones.

Divided into three sections, the book begins by helping new writers understand the importance of laying a solid foundation mentally and organizationally before hitting the paper. The section highlights how to overcome doubts about writing, which tools to use, making time to write amidst a busy schedule, and setting achievable goals. The book then segues into building your brand and promoting yourself as a writer through a self-hosted website, networking, social media, and grassroots marketing and public relations.

"I wanted the book to attract and to be a reference for writers of all levels," says Jones. "One of the challenges I aimed to address was the marketing side for those writers who I have come across repeatedly who are good writers, but not good marketers. The book helps to change that."

Jones draws from his experiences as the former head of a successful branding company he founded, as a writer, and as the editor-in-chief of a pair of magazines to show how any writer can become a marketing master, better promote themselves, and inevitably sell more books.

"When it's all said and done, yes, we write for ourselves first and foremost, but we want to be known, we want to be recognized," Jones says. "I was told that writing is 5 percent of the work and marketing is 95 percent. I know this to be true, and having the right tools at our disposal makes that meeting that 95 percent task possible."

If you're interested in speaking with Chris Jones about topics related to writing, publishing, self-promotion of authors, or authorship, reach him at chris@chrisjonesink.com

###

About the Author:

Chris Jones is a three-time award-winning Virginia Press Association journalist and graphic designer, writer and ghostwriter, magazine editor, and podcast host (The Art & Business of Writing on iTunes). He has been featured in *The Health Journal, Fredericksburg Parent, Richmond Magazine, Coastal Virginia Magazine, CoVA Business, The Local Scoop,* and others.

More About The Book:

The Art & Business of Writing: A Practical Guide to the Writing Life by Chris Jones was released on December 25, 2015. *The Art & Business of Writing*—ISBN 978-0692603703—has 172 pages and is being sold as a trade paperback for $9.99 and on Kindle format for $4.99 on Amazon.

Sample Facebook Group Rules

Below is a sample of Facebook Group rules I used for a community I once managed. This shows you how you can create solid guidelines for governing your group.

Self-Pub Superstars

Welcome, Superstar!

We're here to support and inspire self-published authors so we can write, publish, promote, and sell our work with maximum effectiveness.

Here is how this group works:

1. Writing is hard work and we're here to support one another. Let's keep our comments constructive.
2. Spamming won't be tolerated, and promotional posts will ONLY be allowed inside designated posts when

prompted for you to share your promos, offers, links, social media links, opt-ins, surveys, programs, website links, etc. NO live streaming (Facebook Live videos) is allowed unless approved by admins.

- If we see something that looks like a promotion, we reserve the right to delete it.)
- Since I help coach writers and offer author services, I'll share live videos and info about my programs and offerings. If you're not good with that, then I ask that you not request to join.
- If you break these rules, you may be kicked out of the Sub-Pub Superstars without warning!

3. DO post about your writing challenges, your WIP, and ask for tips, help, or feedback.
4. DO connect and collaborate, share your ideas, discuss the industry openly, and engage with the other members of the group.

If you think you might need extra support, then schedule a 30-minute author strategy session at calendly.com/chrisjonesink

Be sure to listen to my podcast, *The Art & Business of Writing* and get more writing advice at chrisjonesink.com

I'm excited to have you here.

Let's rock!

Chris Jones
Founder, Chris Jones Ink

Theme Days

- **Motivated Monday:** What writing goals do you have for the week?
- **Tip Sheet Tuesday:** Share tools, techniques, and trends in writing, marketing, and publishing you're using to up your author game.
- **Workspace Wednesday:** Let's have a little Hump Day fun. Share a photo of your workspace, or something in your workspace that's inspiring.
- **Table Topics Thursday:** Talk about your current work in progress and what challenges you may be having. Get advice from fellow members about publishing, design, or marketing. Ask questions and share your experiences with writers trying to make a living with their work.
- **Freestyle Friday:** Every superstar needs to promote. Ask for reviews, share a recent blog post, promote your book, ask for Fan Page Likes or invite members to your virtual launches.
- **Celebration Saturday:** What were your wins from the week and how will you celebrate them?
- **Superstar Sunday:** Do you know another rockin' writer we can bring into the fold to make the group more awesome? Invite them to join?

About the Author

Chris Jones is an award-winning journalist and magazine editor, and founder of Chris Jones Ink, a writing studio focused on book publishing, and magazine and web content development.

Throughout his journalism career, Chris has interviewed notable celebrities like HGTV personality Sabrina Soto, Food Network star Rachael Ray, and Daphne Maxwell Reid from *The Fresh Prince of Bel-Air*, and many others. He has authored two books and has ghostwritten and collaborated on five other books and helped over a dozen authors publish their books.

On his podcast, *The Art & Business of Writing*, he has interviewed bestselling authors, marketing and media experts, and other players in the publishing ecosystem.

When not writing or editing, he loves playing retro video games, reading, and experimenting with personal development. He lives with his wife and children in Virginia.

Visit chrisjonesink.com to learn more about him.

www.ingramcontent.com/pod-product-compliance
Lightning Source LLC
Chambersburg PA
CBHW060503280326
41933CB00014B/2849